NorthParadePublishing

©2015 North Parade Publishing Ltd.
4 North Parade,
Bath BA11LF. UK
Printed in China.
www.nppbooks.co.uk

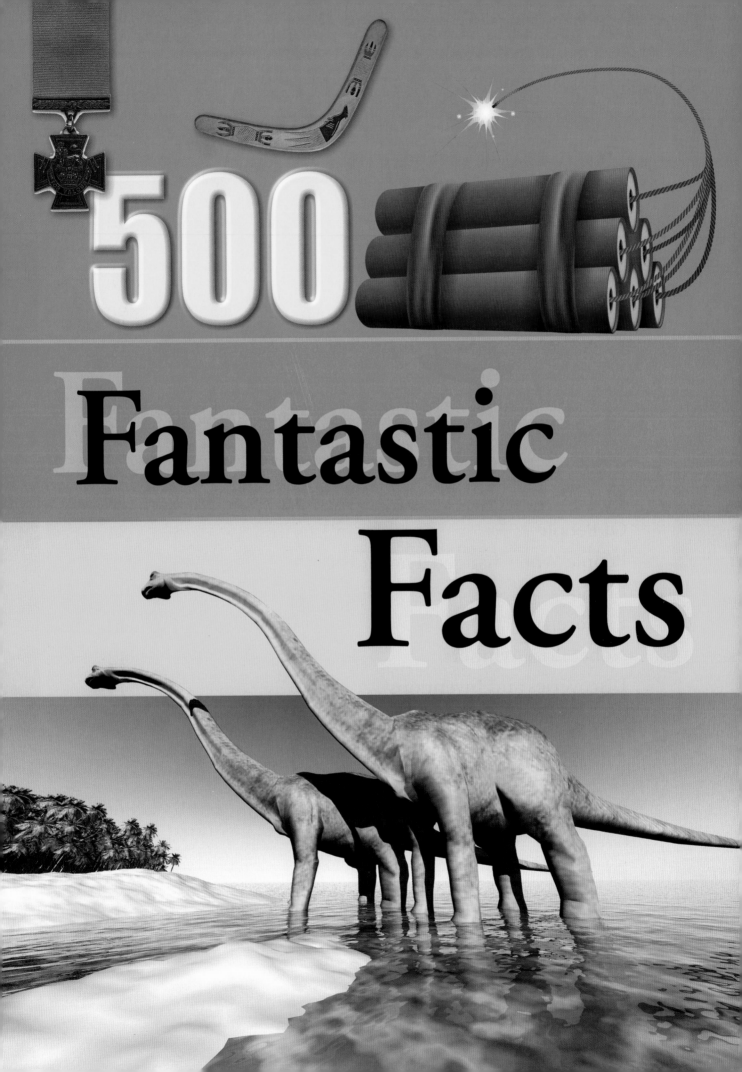

# 500 Fantastic Facts

# Contents

# The Solar System

**1** Do you know how old our solar system is? If it were celebrating its birthday, it would be its 4.6 billionth one now!

**2** Mercury was named after the roman god messenger, who wore winged sandals and was known for his speed. The planet was so named, as it seemed to move faster than the other planets!

**3** Jupiter, the biggest of all the planets, is so big that a thousand Earths' can fit in it! What is also interesting is the fact that the largest planet of our solar system has the shortest planetary day – just 9 hours.

**4** Did you know that the 'ringed' planet Saturn has relatively less mass. Yes, Saturn is made up mostly of hydrogen and helium, the two lightest elements in the universe.

**5** Who had the honour of giving Pluto its name? A scientist? A famous astronomer? No. Pluto was named by an eleven-year-old schoolgirl from the UK, Venetia Burney in 1930.

**6** You already know that the core of the Sun is the hottest place in the solar system. But did you know that the Sun alone accounts for 99.86% of the mass of the whole Solar System?

**7** All the 27 moons of Uranus have been named after characters from William Shakespeare's plays or Alexander Pope's poem The *Rape of the Lock*. So, all the universe's a stage!

**8** All of us know that the Moon is Earth's satellite. But how did the moon form? The Moon formed out of the Earth! Scientists believe that a huge object (probably as big as Mars) hit our Earth 4.5 billion years ago which resulted in a part of the land breaking up and being ejected into space.

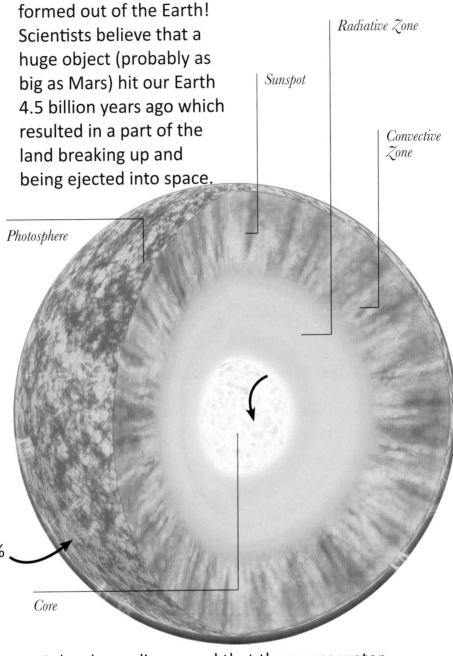

*Radiative Zone*

*Sunspot*

*Convective Zone*

*Photosphere*

*Core*

**9** It has been discovered that there was water on Mars! So the stories about there being life on Mars and aliens visiting Earth could be true!

# Comets, Asteroids and Meteors

**10** You have probably heard of Halley's Comet, but do you know how the comet got its name? It is named after Edmond Halley who not only discovered the comet but also proved to the world that comets move in orbits, which made it easier for people to calculate when the comets could be sighted again.

**11** Mark Twain was born in 1835 and Halley's Comet was also sighted that same year. Twain strongly believed that his fate was dependent on the comet. Incredibly, the year 1910, when Halley's Comet was sighted again after 1835, was also the year when Twain died!

**12** The first asteroid to be discovered was Ceres. This asteroid is so large that it is considered a dwarf planet. It is an amazing fact that the largest asteroid also happens to be the smallest dwarf planet.

**13** The largest asteroid to be visited by a spacecraft is 253 Mathilde. Just like Ceres, this asteroid can also be found in the asteroid belt.

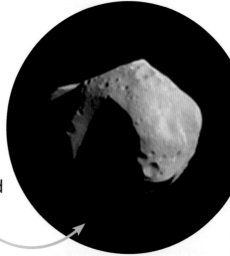

**14** Toutatis is an asteroid named after the Celtic god. It passes the Earth every four years and is one of the few space objects to regularly fly close to the Earth!

**15** Meteoroids are constantly falling to Earth – almost 4 billion of them fall to Earth every day. But the chance of a meteorite (when a meteoroid hits the Earth, it's called a meteorite) hitting any human is... once in every 180 days! The probability of winning the lottery is higher!

**16** These days, anything can be bought and sold. All one needs to know is the art of selling. But a meteorite - can it be sold? Yes! Log on to eBay and see for yourself.

**17** Did you know that the last mass extinction that destroyed 85% of the species on the Earth, (including the dinosaur) occurred when an asteroid hit the Earth? The impact changed global climatic conditions so much that most creatures inhabiting the planet could not survive.

# Galaxies and Stars

**18** Did you know that the word galaxy comes from 'gala' the Greek word for milk? Why would they choose to use this word? It was because when people looked through telescopes, galaxies appeared as 'milky', 'cloudy' areas. Well that justifies the name 'Milky Way' for our galaxy!

**19** The largest natural arrangement in space is a huge wall of galaxies. You might be wondering how long is this large configuration? Well, it is 1.37 billion light years long (and 9.4 trillion kilometres make just one light year)!

**20** Talking about large formations, the largest galaxy, Abell 2029, is so big that its diameter is 80 times bigger than that of our Milky Way! And Abell is as bright as two trillion (2,000,000,000,000) suns put together!

**21** You've seen spiral wire on notebooks but did you know that even galaxies could have a spiral shape too? The largest of them is Malin 1, named after Anglo-Australian astronomer David Malin who discovered it in 1986.

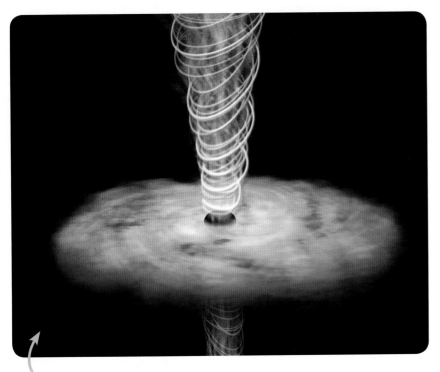

**22** 'Twinkle twinkle little star'... however stars are anything but little. They appear small because they are so far away from us. You will be amazed to know that Betelgeuse (also known as Alpha Orionis), the largest star known to us, has a diameter of 700 million kilometres – 500 times greater than that of the Sun!

**23** What are quasars? Quasars are radio galaxies (galaxies that give out a large amount of radio energy). They are the brightest objects we know in the Universe.

**24** In space, light travels at a speed of almost 300,000 km every second. You can imagine how far the stars are from us if light from the closest star has take over 4 years at this speed to reach us! If you ever want to travel to the stars, it would take you over 70,000 years at the fastest speeds we can currently go!

**25** Jupiter has some weighty issues – it is heavier than all of the other planets put together! And its gravitational pull is such that it absorbs most of the comets and meteors that happen to fly past.

# Telescopes

**26** The largest space telescope is NASA's Hubble Space Telescope which weighs 11 tonnes and is 13.1 metres long! On 24th April 2012, it would have spent 22 years in space!

**27** Do you know which is the highest resolution optical telescope in the world? It is the Swedish 1-metre Solar Telescope on La Palma in the Canary Islands. It uses a mirror in the path of the sunlight that alters its shape a thousand times in a second to compensate for any atmospheric changes.

**28** Did you know when the first telescopes were made? As far back as 1608! These early telescopes were made by Dutch optician Hans Lippershey. Galileo made his telescope soon after and discovered Jupiter's moon.

**29** The world's second largest optical telescopes are the Keck I and II telescopes at the Mauna Kea Observatory in Hawaii, USA. Opened between 1992 and 1996, these telescopes are situated on top of a 4000 metre high mountain. The two telescopes work together to form a single astronomical interferometer.

**30** Do you know the name of the world's largest radio telescope? It is called ALMA, an acronym for Atacama Large Millimetre/Sub-millimetre Array. It is situated on the Chajnator Plateau in the Chilean Andes at a height of 5000 metres above sea level.

**31** La Palma, Canary Islands, Spain is famous not only for the highest resolution telescope but also for the largest optical telescope in the world – the Gran Telescopio Canaris, or GTC. It was inaugurated by King Juan Carlos I of Spain on 24th July 2009.

**33** Did you know that the Greenwich Meridian (also known as the Prime Meridian) passes through an observatory? Yes, it does, through the Royal Observatory founded by King Charles in 1675, but too much light pollution in the city reduced the efficiency of the observatory. In 1884, the GM was defined as 0° for all measurements of longitude.

**32** Did you know that a telescope featured in a James Bond film? The giant 305 metre dish of the Arecibo Observatory in Puerto Rico features in the final shots of the film 'Goldeneye'.

# Flight to Space

**34** The first animal to sit in a rocket and be launched (although not into space) was Albert 1 in 1948, a male rhesus monkey. He and his successor Albert 2, who was the first monkey in space, passed away during these tests.

**35** The first animal to orbit after being launched was Laika, a female husky. She was sent on Sputnik 2 on 3rd November 1957. They did not know how to bring her back, so after ten days in orbit, Laika died.

**36** 'That's one small step for man, but one giant leap for mankind.' Those were the words of Neil Armstrong, the first man to land on the moon, as he stepped out of Apollo 11 on 20th July 1969. Armstrong was accompanied by fellow astronaut Edwin 'Buzz' Aldrin.

**37** Do you know the name of NASA's first space shuttle? You probably know the name, but you might not know that it was NASA's first space shuttle. Columbia was its name and it made its first flight on 12th April 1981. It was destroyed on its 28th mission on 1st February 2003 while re-entering the Earth's atmosphere killing all the seven crew members on board.

## 38

The largest objects (not the heaviest) to be transported by air, were the space shuttles! These almost 122-feet long shuttles were piggy-backed on modified Boeing 747's and transported from their landing sites to Cape Canaveral in Florida.

## 39

Have you ever wondered how astronauts use the washroom in space? Well, they have to strap their thigh and feet so that they stay 'grounded' on the seat. Solid waste is stored on the shuttle until it lands whereas liquid waste is let out into space!

## 40

The first man in space was Yuri Gagarin of the Soviet Union. He spent 1 hour 48 minutes in space on board Vostok 1. The first and also the youngest woman in space was Valentina V Tereshkova (also of the Soviet Union). She spent 2 days, 22 hours, 50 minutes and 8 seconds in space!

## 41

On vacation in space? Yes, that's right, American Dennis Tito was the first space tourist and paid 20 million dollars for his Russian Soyuz flight to the International Space Station.

## 42

Do you know who was the first person to walk in space? Edward H White II made a 36 minute spacewalk from Gemini 4 on June 3rd, 1965.

# Our Earth

**43** Our Earth doesn't take 24 hours to complete one rotation, but 23 hours 56 minutes and 4 seconds, and so 365.2564 days to complete one revolution. That's why we celebrate an extra day every leap year!

**44** The Earth has often been hit by meteors and these meteors can leave huge craters on the surface of the Earth. The biggest of such craters, is the Vredefort Dome, 100 kilometres southwest of Johannesburg. It was voted as South Africa's seventh World Heritage site in 2005.

**45** Do you know why our Earth is called the Blue Planet? That is because when seen from space, out Earth looks like a huge, blue ball. And where does the Earth get its blue colour from? From the water which reflects the blue light of the sky above.

**46** How big can a rock be? As big as a car or a building, maybe? You would be wrong! The biggest rock is 335 metres high, 3.6 kilometres long and 2 kilometres wide. Made of sandstone, Uluru was formerly known as Ayers Rock but the aborigines of Australia gave their sacred rock its new name.

**47** You know that the Moon is the Earth's natural satellite. You probably also know many other facts related to the Earth's satellite, but did you know that the Moon is a million times drier than the Gobi Desert?

**48** The Earth is big, very big! But just how big is big? If numbers interest you, then you would be surprised to know that the total surface area of the Earth is 197 million square miles!

**49** The word "Arctic" comes from the ancient Greek Arktikos, which means the country of the great bear. But the Greeks had no idea if polar bears existed in that region. They gave it the name because of the constellation Ursa Major, the Great Bear, found in the Northern Sky.

**50** If you see the first light of the Sun at 7am in the morning, it actually left the Sun at 6:51:57. It takes eight minutes and three seconds for light to travel the distance to the Earth.

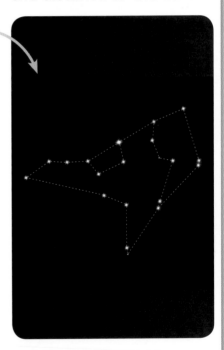

**51** If you ever got inspired from Jules Verne's 'A Journey to the Centre of the Earth' and wanted to travel to the core, you would have to travel a total distance of 6378 kilometres!

# Land Features

**52** You may have seen in movies that when someone gets lost in a desert, they cannot see anything in sight except for sand! Well, for some that's true. A desert is a large area of barren land – and the largest of them is the Sahara Desert in North Africa covering an enormous area of 9,100,000 square kilometres.

**53** All of us know that the highest mountain in the world is Mount Everest. But where did it get its name from? Well, it is named after Sir George Everest, the Surveyor General of India who led the survey that gave Peak XV the status of the highest mountain of the world and the name Mount Everest.

**54** That was about the highest mountain. But do you know which is the longest mountain range in the world? 7, 242 kilometres long, the Andes in South America is the longest mountain range in the world.

**55** All the continents were once a part of one huge landmass. Over millennia, this landmass broke into pieces and those pieces are now the continents we live in.

Did you know that the Earth is still breaking up? The Rift Valley that divides Kenya down the length of the country is an example of this continuous process! Thousands of years in the future, this will lead to the origin of yet another continent.

**56** Did you know that some of the Scottish Highlands are formed from the oldest mountains in the world – some of them are at least 400 million years old!

**57** Did you know that no trees can grow in the Arctic tundra? They can't, because the tundra has a permanently frozen subsoil which is known as permafrost.

**58** Do you know how low is the lowest point on Earth? It is 1302 metres below sea level. And do you know where the lowest point is? It is the Dead Sea, located in the Jordan Rift Valley!

**59** Some of us eat to live and some of us live to eat! In any case, all of us need to eat and with so many people in the world today, we need to produce a lot of food. But in reality, only 11 per cent of the surface of the Earth is used for growing food.

**60** Antarctica has a hat-trick of extremes – it is the highest, the driest and the coldest continent in the world!

# Water Bodies

**61** The Nile is the longest river in the world. 6,695 kilometres long, it flows through Burundi, Dem, Republic of Congo, Egypt, Eritrea, Ethiopia, Kenya, Rwanda, Sudan, Tanzania and Uganda.

**62** Do you know which is the highest waterfall in the world? Three times the size of the Eiffel Tower, the Angel Falls in Venezuela is the highest waterfall – the water drops a distance of 979 metres!

**63** Have you heard of the Great Lakes? The Great Lakes are a group of five freshwater lakes – Superior, Huron, Michigan, Erie and Ontario – in North America on the border between the USA and Canada.

**64** Did you know that the Caspian Sea is not a sea but a lake? This makes the Caspian Sea the world's largest body of inland water. If you poured the entire content of the Caspian Sea away, over Niagara Falls, it would take 400 years to empty!

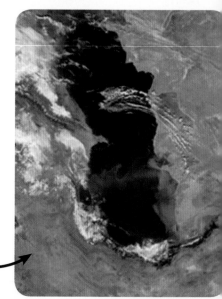

**65** You know that the Nile is the longest river but do you know the name of the largest river? It is the Amazon. The outflow of the Amazon is so great that it can fill almost two million baths every second.

**66** You know tides can be low and tides can be high, but do you know how big the difference between them can be? As much as 16.6 metres in the case of the Bay of Fundy.

**67** Time for some numbers now. About 97% of the water found on Earth is seawater, which means that only 3% is fresh water. Out of this 3%, 2% is frozen in ice sheets and glaciers. This means that the fresh water in lakes and rivers is only 1% of our total water reserve!

2%

97%

1%

**68** Did you know that Amazon river has a 'sibling'! An underground river appears to be flowing 13,000 feet beneath it!

**69** Lake Bosumtwi in Ghana has a very interesting origin. A meteorite hit the earth which formed a crater. Water kept flowing into the crater until the lake was finally formed!

# Islands, Reefs etc.

**70** We all know of the largest landmass surrounded by water. But did you know that it is so large that it is considered a continent and not an island? It is Australia, but because it is not considered an island, the crown of the largest island on Earth goes to Greenland.

**71** Talking of islands, do you know the name of the smallest island with a country status? Well, it is Pitcairn, with an area of just 4.53 square kilometres!

**72** Residents of two 'sister' islands – Tristan de Cunha and St. Helena – live around 2000 kilometres away from each other. This is as far as London is from Moscow!

**73** The Grand Canyon in Arizona is the largest land gorge. It is 1.6 kilometres deep and the width varies from 0.5 kilometres to 29 kilometres. Now, that's quite large!

**74** Did you know that even the youngest island is probably older than you? The island of Surtsey, off the south coast of Iceland, was formed on 14th November 1963!

**75** Now you know the name of the youngest island, but do you know the name of the oldest island? Madagascar, in the Indian Ocean, became an island almost

80 to 100 million years ago when it broke away from the Indian subcontinent.

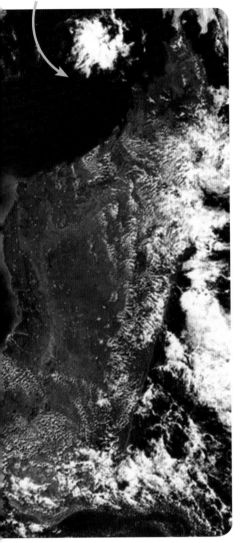

**77** The largest artificial reef is the USS Oriskany which is also called the 'Great Carrier Reef'. Why? Because it was created using the USS Oriskany, the US Navy's attack aircraft carrier which was sunk in the Gulf of Mexico after many years of service.

**78** Have you heard of atolls? An atoll is a coral island or a group of them which encircles a lagoon (very shallow sea water or brackish water) partially or completely. Havadhu Atoll contains 255 islands and covers an area of 2,900 sq kilometres!

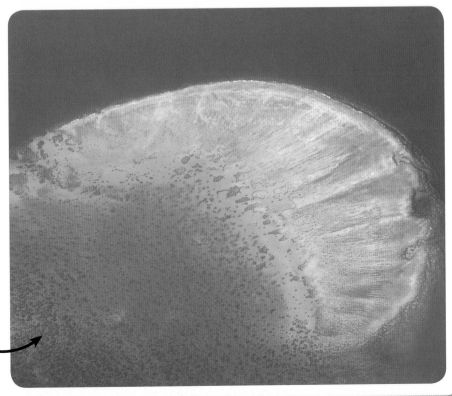

**76** The Great Barrier Reef is the longest reef in the world. At 2,027 kilometres long, this reef is the largest marine structure formed by living creatures. Why do we say living? Because the reef consists of countless billions of dead and live corals!

# Natural Disasters

**79** It is believed that the volcanic eruption from the Greek island Santorini in 1450 B.C. was one of the most powerful ever!

**80** How much damage can a hurricane cause? Well, a lot! It is estimated that Hurricane Katrina that hit the coast of Louisiana and surrounding states on 29th August 2005 caused damage as high as 156 million dollars! It is one of the costliest natural disaster ever!

**81** Did you know that the first recorded evidence of floods caused by China's Huang Ho (also known as the Yellow River) goes back to 2297 B.C.! And since then, the river has flooded at least 1500 times!

**82** Do you know at what speed an avalanche can travel? At 400 kph! Yes, the avalanche caused by the eruption of Mount St Helens volcano on 18th May 1980 travelled at that speed!

**83** Volcanic eruptions can be so deadly that they have been known to bury entire cities! The cities of Pompeii and Herculaneum were buried forever after Mount Vesuvius erupted in 79 AD. Pompeii was found only years later in 1749 and that was by chance!

**84** A blizzard continued for a week – from 3rd to 9th February 1972 and dumped more than 10 feet of snow across various parts of rural Iran. It killed many people but also ended a four-year long drought.

**85** Do you know that the earthquake that occurred under the Indian Ocean on 26th December 2004 resulted in a tsunami that inundated the coastlines of nine countries around the ocean!

**86** Have you heard of the Winter of Terror? It was a period when a series of 649 reported avalanches thundered through the Swiss, Austrian and Italian Alps on 20th January 1951. It is estimated that a record 45,000 people were trapped under the snow.

**87** The most powerful earthquake recorded in recent times is the Valdivia earthquake (also known as the Great Chilean Earthquake) that occurred on 22nd May 1960. On the moment magnitude scale (MMS), it measured 9.5.

# Natural Phenomena

**88** Do you know where is the windiest place in the world? Commonwealth bay in Antarctica. It has recorded windy days consistently and some winds have reached 320 kph. But an individual incidence of fastest wind speed – 408 kph – was recorded at Barrow Island, Australia.

**89** Sometimes the oddest things happen at the strangest of places! Would you expect a snowstorm in the Sahara Desert? Don't be surprised. There was one on 18th February 1979!

**90** How would you like it if it rained almost every day? Believe it or not, it rains up to 350 days a year at Mt Waialeale, Kauai, Hawaii, USA! Only fifteen dry days, !

**91** Do you know that the poles – the South Pole and the North Pole – go without sunshine for almost half the year? The former for 182 days and the latter for 176 days.

**92** Deforestation is serious, but sometimes nature doesn't help either. This is because a storm that hit France on 26-27th December 1999 felled a record 270 million trees!

**93** A single bolt of lightning killed 68 jersey cows that were resting under a tree in Australia on 31st October 2005. Lesson learnt – in case of thunder and lightning, never take shelter under a tree!

**94** What is the hottest place that you can think of on Earth? The cooking range or the fireplace? The hottest place is hotter than both combined. For a fraction of second, the air around a lightning strike heats up to 30,000° C (54,000 ° F)!

**95** When it rained, have you ever recorded how much rain fell? Well, the meteorological departments does! And they recorded a maximum of 26,461 mm of rain in Cherrapunji, Assam, India between 1st August 1860 and 31st July 1861.

Cherrapunji

# Changing Planet

**96** Do you know how much sea levels have changed in the last century? On an average, sea levels have risen about 17 centimetres – but what is interesting is that the rate of increase in just the last decade is almost double of that of the entire last century!

**97** It is easy for us to look at our watches to check the time, but we are not the first to be able to tell the time. Sundials were being used in Egypt as early as 1500–1300 B.C.! Quite some time ago!

**98** Why do we have different time zones? Because the Earth is constantly rotating on its axis, if all of us set our clocks to the same time, midnight would be in the middle of the night on one side of the globe and during the day on the other side!

**99** What can be a greater indication of the growing world than the fact that there are 133 million births each year - 247 births every minute! To break it down even further, that's four babies every second.

**100** Did you know that deserts are not made of sand alone? Many of us may have thought so but the reality is that 85% of the deserts are made up of rocks and gravel. The Sahara Desert, which covers most of Northern Africa, is so big that it is almost as large as China or the United States!

**101** Early scientists believed that the Earth was round. But further studies have shown that the Earth is not round but an oblate spheroid shape. It is slightly flattened at both the poles.

**102** Earthquakes have been occurring ever since the Earth was formed, but their numbers have increased significantly over the years. There are over a million earthquakes in a year, and thousands of them are not even recorded.

**103** The world is getting hotter day by day and many say that the Death Valley is the hottest place on the Earth – consistently hot! But the crown of hottest recorded temperature goes to Azizia in Libya. It recorded 57.8° C on 13th September, 1922.

# Global Warming

**104** We all know it is happening - Global Warming is a fact. The last two decades of the 20th century were the hottest in 400 years and believe it or not, the last eleven out of twelve years have been the hottest since 1850!

**105** We all know that the Arctic ice is melting due to global warming. But did you know that researchers have predicted that the Arctic will experience its first ice-free summer in 2040 or even earlier!

**106** Yes, the glaciers are melting too. Montana's Glacier National Park, which had 150 glaciers in 1910, has only 27 left now! If things don't change drastically, they will soon need to change the name of the park because there wouldn't be any glaciers left!

**107** Three 'tions' are responsible for global warming – industrializa-tion, deforesta-tion and pollu-tion! If we manage to shun these three 'tions' we might be able to save our world from destruction!

**108** Your answer to the 'tions' should be three 'R's – reduce, reuse and recycle. That's the minimum you can do to save our Earth.

**109** Did you know that the golden toad (Bufo periglenes) and the harlequin frog (Atelopus varius) of Costa Rica are no more, all because of global warming!

**110** And the once numerous polar bears in the Hudson Bay area of Canada are now more rare, all because of global warming again. The ice breaks up almost two weeks before it should which reduces the polar bears' hunting time.

**111** Scientists believe that if we do not take measures to control global warming, by 2050, we would be living on a very different planet. Diseases that have been dead for years would resurface and the plants that could save us would be gone! Do your bit now, start by planting a tree.

# Of People

**112** Do you know the name of the world's tallest living human being? His name is Sultan Kosen and he is the 8 feet 3 inches tall! It goes without saying that not only his clothes but his also his shoes are custom made!

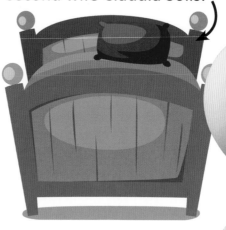

**113** All this jewellery and more will be too little for Elaine Davidson. Why? Because with 4,225 piercings, Elaine is the most pierced person in the world. She ran a cafe in Edinburgh before she dedicated her life to piercings.

**114** A bed is meant to be slept in, right? Not always! Mexico's Manuel Uribe, world's heaviest living man used it as his wedding seat! Manuel is so heavy that he is bed bound and had to be transported with his bed in a truck to the wedding venue when he married his second wife Claudia Solis.

**115** How about some drawings on your body? Well, you may have often seen people with a tattoo here and a tattoo there, but you would be surprised to know that Julia Gnuse has around 95% of her body covered in tattoos! But that's not enough for some – Lucky Diamond Rich has his entire body tattooed in black and then re-tattooed in white.

**116** Talking about whacky things, do you know that Andrew Dahl of USA inflated 23 balloons using only his nose in just three minutes? Well, that's a world record!

**117** And if the last one didn't surprise you enough, wait until you read this. Rob Thomson travelled a distance of 12,159 kilometres from Leysin in Switzerland to Shanghai in China on his skateboard!

**118** Not everyone likes to do things by themselves. Some do strange things in groups, such as the 99 people who assembled at the Millennium Bridge in London dressed as Star Trek characters! The occasion – to celebrate the arrival of MMORPG Star Trek Online. And yes, this too is a world record!

**119** Not everyone does whacky things. Some people are special for doing regular ordinary jobs in the most extraordinary ways or age. Like Bette Calman. At 83, Bette is the oldest female yoga teacher. Three cheers for healthy living!

# People Who Changed The World

**120** You must have heard of and read about Mohandas Karamchand Gandhi, popularly known as Mahatma Gandhi. He is one of the biggest exponents of peace and non-violence and brought freedom to India using these two tools. But did you know that he was never awarded the Nobel Peace Prize even though he was nominated for it a total of five times!

**121** Did you know that Martin Luther King Jr was born Michael King Jr because his father was called Michael King. In fact, he was born Michael King Jr, lived as Michael King Jr and died as Michael King Junior. There is no evidence to support his common name!

"MA VIE EST MON MESSAGE"

"MY LIFE IS MY MESSAGE"

**122** We all know about Nelson Mandela and his fight against apartheid. We also know that he was the first black president of South Africa. And you may also know that he spent many years in jail. But do you know how many years? Almost 30 years! That's a third of his life!

**123** Abraham Lincoln and John F Kennedy had some striking similarities – both were shot in the head on a Friday, Lincoln was admitted to the Congress in 1846 and Kennedy in 1946. But the most amazing fact is that Lincoln's successor was born in 1808 and Kennedy's was born in 1908 and both were called Johnson.

**124** Churchill was not only known for his characteristic 'V' sign that is still used today, but also for his knowledge and political acumen.

So much so that he was awarded the Nobel Prize for Literature in 1953.

**125** We all have heard of Adolf Hitler and how he changed the world, but there was one thing he never wanted to change and that was his moustache. He used to say, "Do not worry about my moustache. If it is not the fashion now, it will be later because I wear it!"

**126** Newton and his law of gravity have kept us grounded! And most of us have been told that Newton was sitting under an apple tree when an apple fell on his head. But in reality, Newton was staring out of his bedroom window when he saw an apple fall from a tree.

**127** We have grown up reading Shakespeare's plays and we all love them. But no one knows the Bard of Stratford-upon-Avon's actual birthday! And what's more interesting is the fact that majority of his works were published seven years after his death!

**128** Did you know that the man who computerised our lives and who earns US $ 250 per second (start calculating how much he earns in a year) is a college dropout?! If he donates US $ 15 to every person on earth, he will still be left with US $5 million to spend!

# Big Stars

**129** Elizabeth Taylor does not need any introduction, does she? We all know that she was a wonderful actress and a great activist, but did you know that she was the first actress in the US to earn US $ 1 million? She did for her role in Cleopatra (1963).

**130** Sachin Tendulkar seems to be on a 'breaking the records' spree! He has scored most runs and most centuries in ODI matches, most runs and most centuries in test cricket, has achieved highest partnership in ODI matches and is the first player to score 200 runs in a 50-over international. He must be a busy man!

**131** We all love J K Rowling's character, Harry Potter. But do you know that twelve publishers rejected her first book, Harry Potter and the Philosopher's Stone saying that her idea wouldn't sell!

**132** Did you know that David Beckham is so popular that there is a gold-covered bronze statue of him in a Thai Buddhist temple?! So much so for the love of the game.

**133** What was "The Oprah Winfrey Show" called before Oprah became its host? AM Chicago. It was renamed in September 1985 and began broadcasting nationally on 8th September 1986. Oprah's show remained the top talk show for nineteen consecutive seasons.

**134** Do you know the name of the 'King of the Ring', who would 'Swing like a Butterfly and Sting like a Bee'? His name is Cassius Marcellus Clay. Doesn't ring a bell? Perhaps you've heard of Muhammad Ali? It's the same man. The BBC named him the 'Sportsman of the century'.

**135** Princess Diana was allowed to retain the title of 'Princess of Wales' even after her divorce from Prince Charles. This was not common, but it was felt the least the people's princess deserved.

**136** Did you know that the photographs from the first shoot of Norma Jean Dougherty – none other than Marilyn Monroe – sold for $352,000?!

**137** Popularly known as the Black Diamond, as a child, Pele used to stuff his socks with paper to convert them into a makeshift football. Who knew that the boy who played with that 'football' would one day be a member of one of the greatest footballing teams ever!

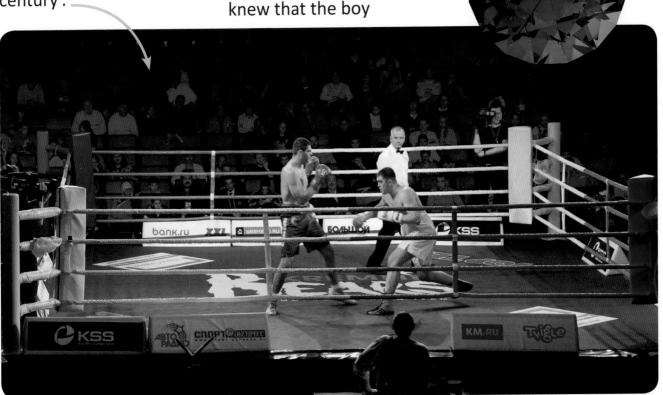

# Explorers

**138** Do you know the name of the Portuguese soldier who took Goa for Portugal? Afonso de Albuquerque, who sailed from Africa to the Indian Ocean, forcibly destroyed Calicut in 1510 and claimed Goa for Portugal the same year.

**139** The Strait of Juan de Fuca is named after the sailor Juan de Fuca who was the first one to travel on that route. But did you know that Juan was a Greek navigator called Apostolos Valerianos who travelled under a Spanish name?

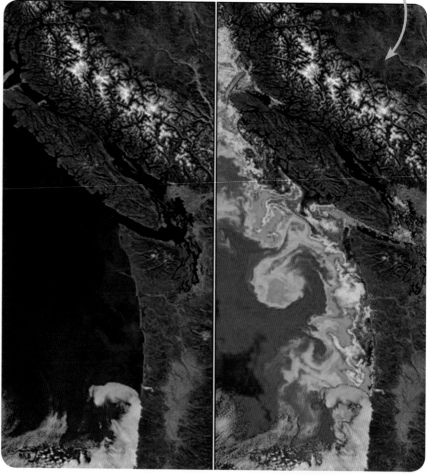

**140** Colonel Yuri Alexeyevich Gagarin was a Soviet cosmonaut (they are called astronauts in the US) and the first human in space. He spent 108 minutes in space on 12th April 1961 on board Vostok 1.

**141** Captain Cook was the first person to map Australia and New Zealand and he also went to Antarctica and Easter Island on his second expedition. But did you know that he was the first person to control the disease scurvy on board of ships? Although he didn't know that scurvy was caused by lack of vitamin C, he offered fresh fruit to his sailors who then got 'miraculously' better.

**142** Whether in fact George Mallory reached the summit of Mount Everest in 1924 but died coming down, is something that will be debated for many years. But officially, the first people to reach the top of the world are Edmund Hillary and Tenzing Norgay.

**143** Have you ever wondered how cold the North Poles is? The first person to experience the chill felt there was Robert Edwin Peary who was allegedly the first person to lead an expedition to the North Pole and reached it in 1909.

**144** Robert Falcon Scott left for an expedition to the South Pole and reached it on 17th January 1912 only to see that Roald Amundsen had already put his flag there on 14th January 1911! And not only that, Roald was also the first person to reach both the poles!

**145** Ferdinand Magellan was a Portuguese explorer who led the first expedition that sailed around the Earth. Out of the original 270 crew members who started the expedition, only 18 managed to get back and unluckily, Magellan was not one of the 18.

**146** Undersea exploration can be fun. It was during one such dive when Jacques-Yves Cousteau, a French undersea explorer, realised the need for a breathing apparatus that supplied oxygen to divers. In 1943, along with engineer Emile Gagnan, Cousteau invented the aqualung, which allowed divers to stay underwater for several hours!

# Nobel Prize Winners

**147** We all know about Nobel prizes and that the prizes were awarded by Alfred Nobel to recognise achievement, but did you know that Alfred Nobel himself held 355 different patents, the most important of them being the patent for dynamite.

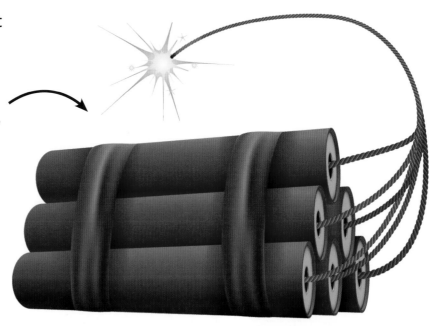

**148** Nobel Prizes are not just named after Alfred Nobel, they were created by him. He left his worth to establish prizes in physics, chemistry, physiology or medicine, literature, and peace to "those who, during the preceding year, shall have conferred the greatest benefit on mankind".

**149** The first recipients of the Nobel peace Prize were John Dunant and Frederic Passy in 1901. Dunant is better known as the founder of the Red Cross and Passy was a French social activist and international arbitrator.

**151** The youngest person to get a Nobel Prize was William Lawrence Bragg. In 1915, along with his father Sir William Henry Bragg, William, then 25 years old, received the prize for advancement in physics. The father and son team were awarded "for their services in the analysis of crystal structure by means of X-rays".

**150** The first woman to be awarded the Nobel Prize was Marie Curie. She got this award for her contribution to the development of chemistry by discovering radium and polonium.

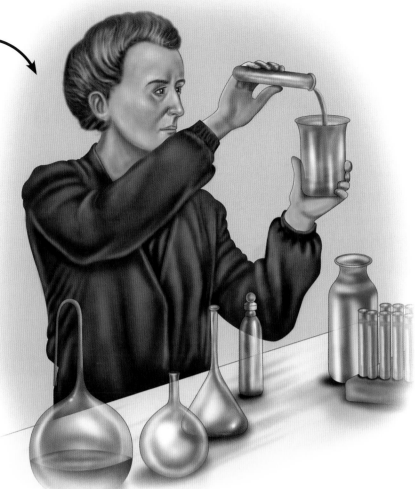

**152** Did you know that Adolf Hitler prevented three German Nobel Laureates – Richard Kuhn, Adolf Butenandt and Gerhard Domagk – from accepting the Nobel Prize?! Later, they did receive the Nobel Prize Diploma and Medal, but they could not get the prize money.

**154** This road sign that you see has Jean-Paul Sartre's name on it. He was a well-known French philosopher, playwright, novelist, screenwriter, political activist, biographer, and literary critic. But he was more known for something that only one other person has done – he refused the Nobel Prize! Not many have done that!

**153** Did you know where Aung San Suu Kyi was when she was awarded the Nobel Peace Prize in 1991 "for her non-violent struggle for democracy and human rights"? In prison! Fighting for the right cause in the right way in Burma.

# Discoveries and Inventions

**155** We have heard of Victoria Falls and some of us may have visited them too. But have you ever thought that for a long time, no one knew of its existence! Yes, not until David Livingstone discovered it in 1855 and named it after Queen Victoria.

**156** Things have been made so simple for us. Every time we fall sick, we take medicine, but imagine when there were no pills! Credit goes to Louis Pasteur and Jules Francois Joubert for demonstrating the effect of antibiotics in 1887.

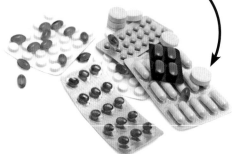

**157** We all love Coca-Cola and many can't imagine a life without it! But before 8th May 1886, there was no Coca Cola. It was on this day that it was sold to the public for the first time in Atlanta as a medicine.

**158** Reaching India had been a wish of many explorers over the years. Columbus tried getting to India and found America instead. Many tried but failed. Then Vasco da Gama travelled round the Cape of Good Hope and up the east coast of Africa and arrived in India on 20th May 1498.

**159** Good bacteria, bad bacteria – we have both. But do you know who discovered bacteria? It was discovered by Antonie van Leeuwenhoek of the Netherlands in 1863.

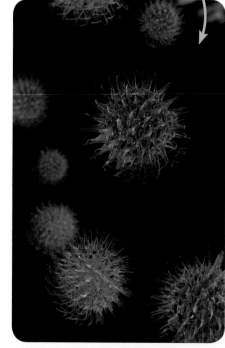

**160** "Eureka! Eureka!" That's what Archimedes shouted when he discovered that any floating object displaces its own weight in fluid, so creating the law of buoyancy.

**161** We all wear jeans but have you ever thought who first made our favourite pair of jeans? Levi Strauss realised that gold miners needed strong trousers and started making them from tent canvas. Eventually he started using denim with rivets to reinforce the seams. It was standard clothing and eventually became favoured by all!

**162** Louis Braille invented Braille – the raised-dot writing system used by the blind – at the age of 15. But that's not surprising. What is surprising is that Louis himself was blind!

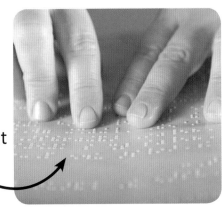

**163** Every time the phone bell rings, remember to thank the Bell behind it – Alexander Graham Bell. In 1886, when means of communication were in their infancy, Bell's invention definitely made the world appear a smaller place.

# Computer Science

**164** The father of the computer is Charles Babbage, who in 1834, tried to build a complicated machine called the analytical engine. He could never complete it but computers today are based on the basic principles laid down by Babbage.

**165** In 1953, International Business Machines (IBM) entered the market with its first digital computer (IBM 701). In 1956, IBM came out with the first hard disk drive and it was around this time that the term 'artificial intelligence' was coined.

**167** In 1964, Douglas Engelbart invented the mouse, you probably know this. But do you know why he named it a 'mouse'? Because the tail came out of the end!

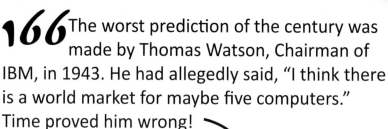

**166** The worst prediction of the century was made by Thomas Watson, Chairman of IBM, in 1943. He had allegedly said, "I think there is a world market for maybe five computers." Time proved him wrong!

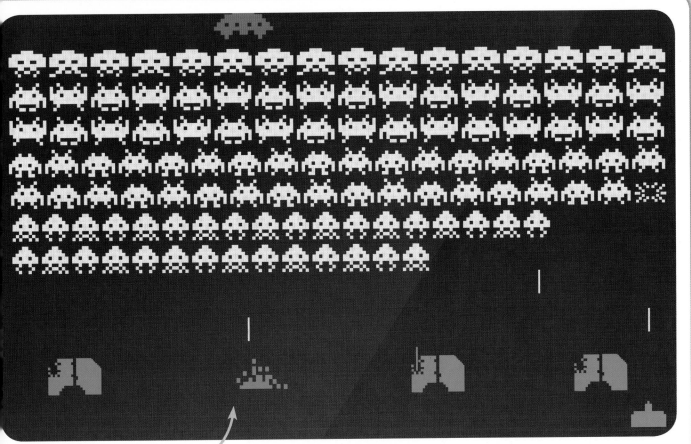

**168** What's the one special thing about the game 'Spacewar'? Well, it is the first ever computer game! It was developed in 1962 by Steve Russell and his team at MIT.

**169** We all know about Apple Computers, Steve Jobs and their successes. We also know that the computers are called 'macs', short for Macintosh. But you probably didn't know that Jef Raskin, an Apple employee, coined this name after his favourite variety of apple.

**170** Alan Shugart with the team at IBM developed the first floppy which IBM released in 1971. They gave it the name 'floppy' because of its 'flexibility'.

**171** Bill Gates called his organisation Micro-soft, a portmanteau of microcomputer and software. But the hyphen was lost during registration and the name stuck.

# The Internet

**172** How heavy can 'G' be? Read on to find out! The development of the internet started as far back as the 1960's at MIT. The first person sent out the message 'LOG'. Why 'log'? He wanted to write login but the network crashed because of the huge load transmitting the letter 'g'!

**173** Sentences on social networking sites and in text messages are supported by emoticons. We can't seem to do without them, but have you ever wondered who created the first emoticon? Kevin Mackenzie in 1979, but it was a simple -). Three years later, ☺ was proposed by Scott Fahlman and has stayed ever since.

**174** Legend has it that Amazon.com became big becau that's the first shopping site the search engine Yahoo would open up. Why? Because back in the times before Google, Yahoo would list sites alphabetically!

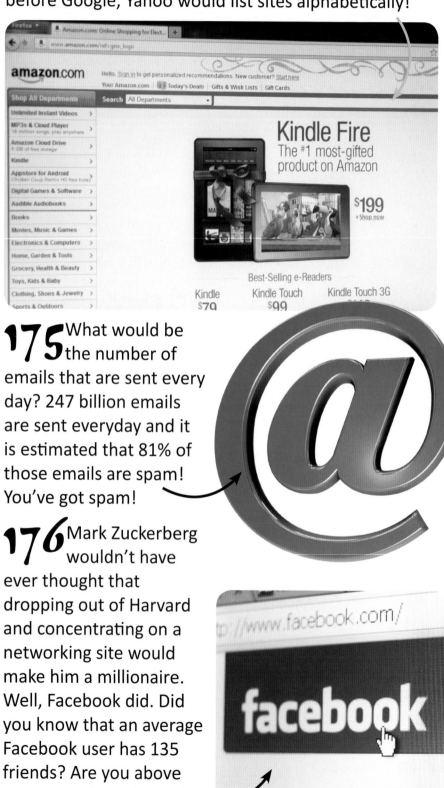

**175** What would be the number of emails that are sent every day? 247 billion emails are sent everyday and it is estimated that 81% of those emails are spam! You've got spam!

**176** Mark Zuckerberg wouldn't have ever thought that dropping out of Harvard and concentrating on a networking site would make him a millionaire. Well, Facebook did. Did you know that an average Facebook user has 135 friends? Are you above average or just friendly?

**177** The first web browser was called Mosaic which was developed at the National Centre for Supercomputing Applications. It was launched in 1993 and discontinued in 1997. Other popular browsers such as Internet Explorer, Google Chrome etc. came much later and retain much of Mosaic's original graphical user interface and interactive experience.

**178** According to CyberAtlas, it took the internet 5 years to reach the 50 million user mark. This is interesting but what is more interesting is the fact that it took television 13 years and the radio 38 years to reach the same mark!

**179** Time for some numbers – 490 million users visit YouTube every month. These people rack up an estimated 92 billion page views every month. It is estimated that we spend a total of 2.9 billion hours on YouTube in a month – this amounts to over 325,000 years!

**180** The Advanced Research Projects Agency Network (ARPANET) was the world's first network that could successfully switch packet data. ARPANET was developed by the US's defence department for their use. ARPANET later led to the development of the Internet which was commercialised in 1995.

# Great Books

**181** The Harry Potter series is a great range of books, but the author is even greater! Harry Potter books have sold more than 400 million copies around the world (and still counting!) and are published in 55 languages.

**182** At 12.67 inches thick, the entire series of Agatha Christie's Miss Marple detective stories (a collection of 12 novels and 20 short stories printed together) is the thickest book and is titled 'The Complete Miss Marple!

**183** According to the Guinness Book of Records, the most banned classic novel is 'The Great Gatsby' written by F Scott Fitzergald in 1924. As recently as 1987, it was challenged again!

**184** Did you know who wrote the first sequel to a book? Daniel Defoe. After the 'Adventures of Robinson Crusoe' became popular, he wrote 'The Farther Adventures of Robinson Crusoe.

**185** Do you like detective stories? If you do, then do you know who wrote the first detective story? Edgar Allen Poe. It was called 'Murders in the Rue Morgue'.

THE
# LIFE
AND
STRANGE SURPRIZING
ADVENTURES
OF
ROBINSON CRUSOE,
Of YORK, MARINER:

Who lived Eight and Twenty Years, all alone in an un-inhabited Island on the Coast of AMERICA, near the Mouth of the Great River of OROONOQUE;

Having been cast on Shore by Shipwreck, where-in all the Men perished but himself.

WITH

An Account how he was at last as strangely deli-ver'd by PYRATES.

*Written by Himself.*

LONDON:
Printed for W. TAYLOR at the Ship in Pater-Noster-Row. MDCCXIX.

**186** What is so special about a copy of Geoffrey Chaucer's book 'The Canterbury Tales'? One of the first ever-printed books, a copy of this book was sold in London for £4,621,500!

**187** Shakespeare has always been a favourite. So much so that someone bought one of the first editions of his works dated 1623, for £4,156,947! So much for the love for literature!

**188** You know that printing and publishing houses publish all your favourite books. But do you know which publishing house has been doing so for the longest time? Cambridge University Press. It has been around since 1534.

**189** The one place where you are most likely to find all your favourite books is the Library of Congress. Founded in 1800, this library has more than 20,000,000 books which makes it the world's largest library!

# Great TV

**190** Did you know that it is estimated that in an average home, the TV is switched on for 7 hours 40 minutes a day? Almost a third of the day!

**194** The first Emmy Awards, the equivalent of the Oscars, was aired for the first time on 25th January 1949.

**191** Talking about medical dramas, do you know which is the longest running prime time medical drama? 'Casualty', (BBC) running since 1986!

**193** Couch potatoes should know this! Which is the most watched TV series? Globally, the medical drama 'House' is the most watched TV serial with more than 81.8 million viewers in 66 countries!

**192** The fastest selling TV formats have been 'Got Talent' and 'X Factor'. Produced by Simon Cowell, the two franchises have been sold around the world. 'Got Talent' was the only show to be no. 1 in the US and the UK at the same time.

**195** An average kid (between 2 and 17 years of age) in the US spends 900 hours a year in school and 1,023 hours in front of the TV!

**196** Do you know why Coronation Street (running since 1960) became the longest running soap opera on TV? Because 'As The World Turns' which was running since 1956 was stopped in 2010.

**197** What were the first words spoken on television? "Good afternoon, ladies and gentlemen. It is with great pleasure that I introduce you to the magic of television..." And the announcer was Leslie Mitchell.

**198** People have always found television for children was popular and in demand. That is the reason the first children's series called 'For the Children' was started way back in 1937!

LONGEST

# Great Cinemas

**199** Do you know who is the most frequently recurring character on TV? Our very own Sherlock Holmes! He has been portrayed by 81 actors in over 217 movies! Elementary, my dear Watson, elementary!

**200** Would it be a surprise if I tell you that the Guinness book of Records states that the highest earning movie stars are Daniel Radcliffe and Emma Watson. You don't need to potter about Harry Potter, do you?

**201** 3D is not new. In 1894, William Friese-Greene became the first man to file a patent for a device that combines two separate pictures in one 3D image.

**202** Avatar and The Dark Knight were in close competition with The Dark Knight losing all of its awards to Avatar, except for one – The Dark Knight is still the highest-grossing movie in its opening weekend.

**203** The most expensive 3D animation movie till date is the 3D version of A Christmas Carol. It took $200 million to produce it, and it got back that and more in receipts!

**204** Best Director Oscars had been the prerogative of male directors until 2008 when Kathryn Bigelow became the first director to get this award for 'Hurt Locker'.

**205** It's official - Guinness records have accepted it! Avatar is the most successful movie in history! It has the top position in the foreign chart, the world chart and the domestic chart!

**206** The highest grossing director ever is Steven Spielberg. His movies have earned more than $ 3.76 billion at the box office. Well worthwhile, bringing back the dinosaurs!

**207** We know that extras work in movies and generally all movies have extras, but not as many as 'Gandhi'. Made in 1982, this movie had a record 294,560 extras! They appeared in the scene showing Gandhi's funeral.

# Great Music

**208** Michael Jackson was not only the most famous living person, he retained his 'most famous' tag even after his death. In the year after his death, a record 11.3 million tracks were downloaded in the US and 2.8 million albums were sold in the UK!

**209** And if you thought that was a lot, wait till you read this – in 1989, Michael Jackson topped the Forbes list as the highest paid entertainer. The record is unbroken to-date!

**210** The first CD single to be brought out by a band was 'Brothers in Arms' in 1985. And you probably know that it was by Dire Straits.

**211** After a hard day's night, and hard work, the Beatles have been named the biggest selling group in the world ever!

**213** Did you know that White Christmas was the world's best selling single for more than fifty years until the prized spot was taken over by Elton John's tribute to Princess Diana 'Candle in the Wind'.

**214** The most charted teenager in the US is the singer and actress Miley Cyrus. She has hits under her own name and also as Hannah Montana.

**215** Madonna's Sticky and Sweet Tour (23rd August 2008 to 2nd September 2009) has been ranked as the most successful tour by a solo artist. Why? Well, because she managed to earn $ 408 million during the tour!

**212** What's special about one particular Rolls Royce Phantom V? Well, the one that was owned by John Lennon of the Beatles was sold at auction in 1985 for $ 2,299,000!

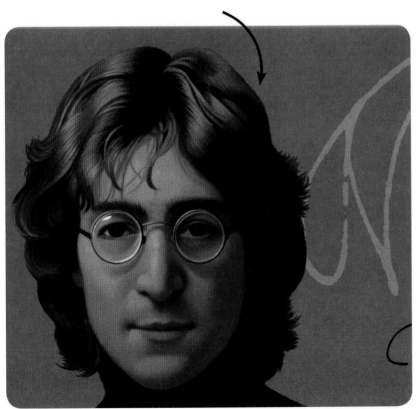

# Great Buildings

**216** Have you heard of Burj Khalifa? Well you should have. Formerly known as Burj Dubai, at 828 metres, Burj Khalifa it is the tallest building ever!

**217** Did you know that the Eiffel Tower was made as a temporary structure for the Universal Exhibition held in Paris in 1889? But it became so popular that it has stayed there ever since.

**218** Angkor Wat in Cambodia is the largest religious structure in the world! It is built over an area of 83,110 sq km.

**219** The biggest lighthouse ever built was the Pharos of Alexandria. It was 124 metres tall. The tallest lighthouse today is in Yamashita Park, Yokohama, Japan. It is 106 metres tall.

**220** Why does the Leaning Tower of Pisa lean? Because soon after the construction started in 1173, the foundation began to sink into the ground on one side. The design was adjusted but in vain. The tilt increases with every passing year but the structure still stands.

**221** It is a space-based myth that the Great Wall of China is the only man made structure visible from the moon and space! It is not visible, but that doesn't reduce the greatness of this 3,460 km long structure which was built around 200 B.C.!

**222** Stonehenge was built in stages from about 3000 B.C. The origin of the stones, how they were transported to the location, and why they were transported there is still a mystery!

**223** There is a London Bridge in London and there is another London Bridge in the US. The one in the US was taken from London – it is the largest structure ever moved and the largest antique ever sold!

# Great Railways

**224** The oldest steam locomotive in use is the Fairy Queen. It was built in 1855 by Kitson Thompson Hewitson. It was restored in 1966 and brought back into service in 1997. When not in use, it can be seen at the Railway Museum in New Delhi, India.

**225** The award for the longest metro and the oldest metro system go to The London Underground. Opened in 1863, it has a combined length of around 400 kilometres.

**226** Which country has the largest rail network? I don't think you need to think a lot about this one – the US has the largest railway network at around 226,427 kilometres!

**227** Tibet is the highest and the biggest plateau and is often called the 'roof of the world', so it isn't a surprise that the Tanggula Railway Station in Tibet is the highest station in the world – it is 5068 metres above sea level.

**228** Do you know what was used as fuel during a coal shortage in Turkestan in 1919? Dried fish! That was the only time a train has been powered by fish.

**229** The Orient Express was the first trans-European train and began trips from Paris to Bulgaria on 5th October 1883. From 1889, it travelled as far as Constantinople (Turkey).

**230** The world's fastest scheduled rail services are the Japanese bullet trains (shinkansen). They were introduced in 1964 when Tokyo was the venue for the Olympic Games.

**232** Have you heard of the trains that don't run on a track? Well, they do exist and are called Maglev (short for magnetic levitation). They do not run on the track but float above it by means of magnetic repulsion.

**231** We all know of the Eurostar and that it ferries passengers between London, Paris and Brussels through the Channel Tunnel. But did you know that in its first decade of service, it carried 59 million passengers?!

# Great Cars

**233** Bugatti Veyron Super Sport is the fastest car in the world and can achieve a speed of 267 miles per hour. For such a high speed, one has to pay a high price – the base price of the car is $ 2,400,000!

**234** The Model T produced by Henry Ford's motor company in 1908 in the US was the first affordable car. Why? Because Henry Ford had designed an 'assembly line' production system which reduced the cost of production considerably!

**235** We all know that the seat belt is mandatory not just for regulations but for our own safety. Do you know which country was the first to realise this? The safty-conscious Czechoslovakia.

**236** The Volkswagen Beetle doesn't need any introduction. Founded by Ferdinand Porsche, it was first manufactured in Germany in 1937. When the production ended in 2003, a total of more than 21,529,463 of Beetles had been made. A new version was produced in 1998.

**237** The Mini was produced in the UK in August 1959. By 2000, more than 5.3 million cars were built. It was the first British car to sell more than a million. Like the Beetle, the old model was discontinued and a new one launched in 2001.

**238** Do you know how Mercedes got its name? It took its name from the daughter of Daimler's then director, Emil Jellinek.

**239** We all know that each Rolls Royce is 'ornamented' with the Spirit of Ecstasy. The only two cars that don't have this hood ornament were Princess Elizabeth's 1950 Phantom IV (she chose the mascot of St. George on horseback slaying a dragon) and Princess Margaret's 1954 Phantom IV (she chose Pegasus).

**240** The first car to reach a speed of 1,228 kph and break the sound barrier is the Thrust SSC. Driven by Royal Air Force pilot Andy Green, this supersonic car set the record in 1997.

**241** What is so special about cars in James Bond movies? Well, are mainly Aston Martins! A bit about Aston Martins – these are luxury sports cars made in the UK since the 1920s.

# Great Aircraft and Aviation Pioneers

**242** The history of aviation starts with the first hot air balloon. The credit for the first hot-air balloon flight goes to the Montgolfier Brothers – Joseph and Étienne. They tested their first unmanned hot air balloon on 5th June 1783.

**243** Soon after the Montgolfier Brothers had made their hot-air balloon, Francois Laurent (Marquis d'Arlandes) and Jean-Francois Pilatre de Rozier took off in a Montgolfier hot-air balloon and travelled about 9 kilometres in 23 minutes! The first men in air!

**244** The Wright Brothers were the first people to make the first controlled, powered and sustained heavier-than-air human flight on 17th December 1903, but did you know that before they built airplane, the Wright Brothers built bicycles!

**245** You may have heard about Amelia Earhart. She was the first woman to fly the Atlantic. After making many flying records, she disappeared during an attempt to fly around the world in 1937.

**246** The Airbus A380 is the world's largest and widest passenger aircraft. It can seat 525 people in a typical three class set and 853 people in an all economy class configuration.

**247** Do you know what is special about the Concorde? It is the only passenger aircraft ever to fly faster than the speed of sound. The Concorde stopped flying in 2004 but can be seen in museums and airports in the US, UK, France, Germany and Barbados.

**248** Do you know what is known as the 'Queen of the Skies'? Another hint – it is also called the 'Jumbo Jet'. Still can't guess? It is the Boeing 747 – the world's most recognizable aircraft and was the first wide-body ever produced.

**249** What is special about the Sea Harrier? Well, it is a VTOL aircraft. This means it can hover, take off and land vertically! Now you know what VTOL stand for – vertical (V) take (T) off (O) and landing (L).

# Great Weapons

**250** We all know that spears are one of the oldest weapons used by humans. But how old? Well, the earliest evidence of humans using spears, dates back about 400,000 B.C. to a part of Germany now near Schöningen.

**251** The atlatl was an ancient spear throwing device! The atlatl was developed in Africa around 40,000 B.C. and the darts it released could kill a deer at a distance of 40 metres!

**252** A boomerangs is another flying weapon and if thrown well they can return. Well, most don't! Nonetheless, the boomerang is a very old weapon associated with Australia's aboriginal people. The oldest boomerang yet is 23000 years old and was found in a cave in Poland. It was made from a mammoth's tusk!

**253** We may know about the revolver but do you know why is it called so? Because it has a revolving chamber. Samuel Colt's revolver is a popular weapon even today.

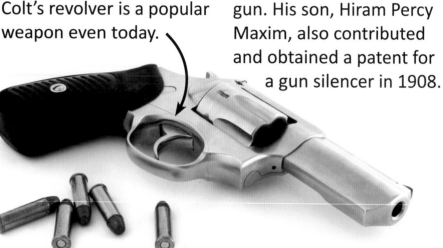

**255** Hiram Steven Maxim contributed to the development of guns by inventing the first machine gun. His son, Hiram Percy Maxim, also contributed and obtained a patent for a gun silencer in 1908.

**254** Nuclear weapons are devastating and they are best unused, but there are two instances when they have been used to-date. The nuclear bomb dropped on Hiroshima on 6th August 1945 was called 'Little Boy' and the one dropped on Nagasaki on 9th August 1945 was called 'Fat Man'.

**256** We have heard that lasers are now used in warfare (in place of radar) for targeting of missiles etc, but did you know that laser is an acronym? It stands for Light Amplification by Stimulated Emission of Radiation.

**257** You know about the AK 47 but if I ask you about the Kalashnikov, you might be confused. Don't be - both are one and same – selective-fire, gas-operated assault rifles.

**258** The Maxim Gun was the first self-powered machine gun. It was developed by Sir Hiram Steven Maxim in 1884.

# Ancient Civilizations

**259** Did you know that the pharaohs in Ancient Egypt would never let their hair be seen? They would wear cloth headdresses, like the one you can see on Tutankhamen's golden mask.

**260** Have you ever noticed that ancient Egyptians appeared to wear a lot of make-up? They did, but not to beautify their faces but to protect themselves from the Sun. They also believed that make-up had healing effects.

**261** We know that the expression 'Achilles' heel' refers to a single weakness in a person, but do you know where this expression originated from? Legend has it that Achilles, the greatest Greek warrior, was dipped in River Styx so that he became immortal. His mother held him by the heel which was the only part of the body that wasn't touched by the water. Years later, a poisonous arrow aimed at his vulnerable heel killed him.

**262** We should thank the Ancient Greeks as they played an important part in the development of the alphabet. In fact, the word 'alphabet' comes from the first two letters of the Greek alphabet – alpha and beta.

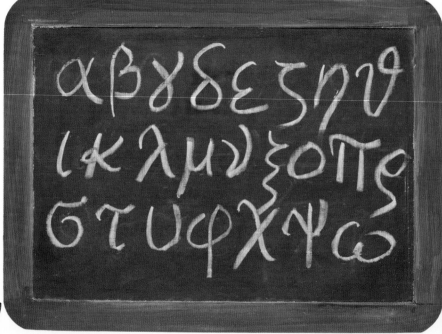

**263** Do you know what was used for writing in Ancient Chinese? Animal bones, turtle shells, silk, or even bamboo slices!

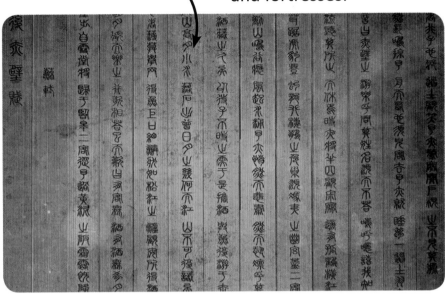

**266** Can you guess why the Incas are called the Romans of the Ancient World? Because like the Romans, they built brilliant roads and fortresses.

**267** Did you know that ancient Roman cavalrymen rode without stirrups? Why? Because stirrups weren't even invented back then!

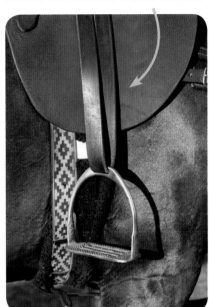

**264** Did you know that the Mayans desired some very special physical characteristics for their children – one of them being crossed eyes! They would dangle objects in front of a newborn's eyes, until they became completely and permanently crossed.

**265** Machu Picchu is the most important Incan city perched high up in the Andes Mountain. Due to its isolation, it escaped the eyes of the Spanish and was discovered only in 1911?

# Ancient Structures

**268** The Sphinx of Giza is the oldest monolith structure believed to have been built at around 2500 B.C. How the nose was destroyed is unknown but some believe that it was the act of Sa'im al-dahr.

**270** The Parthenon was built between 447 and 438 B.C. It had served as a church and as a mosque before it was used as a depot for munitions when the Turkish had occupied Greece. An explosion in 1687 tore through the building and caused much of the damage seen today.

**271** We have all heard of the Colosseum in Rome that was built by Emperor Vespasian between 72–80 AD. But did you know that the southern side of this huge structure with 80 entrances and a seating capacity of 50,000 was destroyed in a massive earthquake?

**269** Contrary to popular belief, the pyramids of Egypt were not all built by slaves. They were built by Egyptians who lived in the surrounding villages and the work was supervised by the pharaoh's men. Graffiti such as "Friends of Khufu", "Drunkards of Menkaure" etc. show that these men were close to the king.

**272** The Mayans are known for their architecture, especially their temples. But do you know what is so special about the temple in Chichen Itza? During the vernal equinox, light and shadow fall on one side of the temple in such a way that it looks like a snake!

**273** Did you know that the present location of the Temple of Abu Simbel is not its original location? This temple of Ramses and his wife Nefertiti was cut into more than 800 pieces and moved to its current location 200 metres away due to the rising waters of the Aswan Dam.

**274** Do you know what the theatre of Pompeii is famous for? Definitely for being the first permanent theatre of Rome, but more for the death of Julius Caesar. It was here that Caesar was murdered in 44 B.C.

**275** Did you know that 95% of the 887 monolithic statues known as Moai on Easter Islands are carved from distinctive solidified volcanic ash or tuff found around the extinct volcano Rano Raraku?

# Wonders of the World

**276** One of the new seven wonders of world, the statue of Christ the Redeemer, is located at the top of Corcovado Mountain in Rio de Janeiro in Brazil. The statue is 38m high and houses a small chapel at the base.

**277** The Taj Mahal, another one of the new seven wonders, is an epitome of love. Situated in Agra, India, the Taj Mahal is a mausoleum built by Emperor Shah Jahan in the loving memory of his wife Mumtaz Mahal.

**278** The largest engineering project in the history of mankind, the Channel Tunnel (also known as the Euro Tunnel), is a rail link under the English Channel between Folkestone and Coquelles that has a capacity of 600 trains one way each day!

**279** Many ancient Greek historians have described this site as the most beautiful in the world, but none of us has ever seen it. Did you guess The Hanging Gardens of Babylon? The Hanging Gardens were supposedly built by King Nebuchadnezzar II around 600 B.C. to please his wife Amytis, but no archaeological evidence of these gardens has been found so far.

**280** Another man-made marvel is the city of Teotihuacan, around 50 kilometres from Mexico City. The city was established around 200 B.C., but no one knows which civilization established it or what was its original name. The current name was given by the Aztecs much later.

**281** Heard of the brilliant sky light displays in the polar regions? These are known as aurora borealis in the north and aurora australis in the southern hemisphere. This wonder of nature is caused by the collision of gaseous particles in Earth's atmosphere with charged particles released from Sun.

**282** Petra is another wonder included in the new seven wonders list. It shows not only the work of man, but also the work of nature – the mausoleums and other monuments surrounded by beautiful red hills are an obvious wonder!

**283** Considered a medieval wonder by many, Hagia Sophia – first a church, then a mosque and now a museum – has passed every test of time – fire, earthquake and even riots! First made in 360 AD, it was restored thrice and additions have been made many times.

**284** Located 35 kilometres east of Xi'an, the Terracotta Warriors and Horses are the most important discovery of the 20th century. These funerary objects were accidently found by the villagers in Lishan Hills around Lintong County in 1974.

# Ancient World History

**285** Before the Romans came to Britain, it was home to a number of tribes. How do we know this? Thanks to a Roman geographer called Ptolemy who wrote a description of Britain and he listed the names of the many British tribes at the time.

**286** Did you know even five thousand years ago trade was flourishing between India and Mesopotamia – between the Indus Valley Civilization and Sumer. And how do we know this? Ancient Mesopotamian text talks about a land called Meluhha and its exotic commodities and their trade, and many Indus objects have been found in Mesopotamia.

**288** What is the Herodium? It is the desert fortress-palace of King Herod the Great built on top of a volcano-like hill with a truncated cone, near the city of Bethlehem. Herod may have even been buried there!

**289** How do we know that the Moabites, a west Semitic people, really existed thousands of years ago and are not a figment of our imagination? It is thanks to the Mesha Stele (Moabite Stone) that was written around 830 B.C., and talks about the Moabites. It was buried around Dhiban (in modern-day Jordan) for centuries until it was accidently discovered in 1868 by a German missionary.

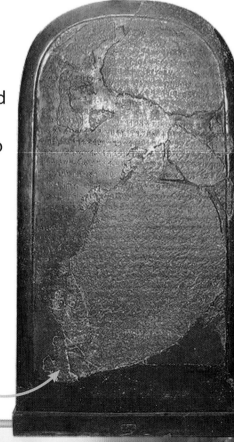

**290** In the honour of the ruler Ptolemy V Epiphanes, an important piece of work was created and engraved in 196 B.C. It was uncovered in the 18th century and paved the way for researchers to decipher ancient Egyptian writings. What is it? The Rosetta Stone!

**294** The ruins of the Indus Valley Civilization were discovered only in the 1920's, thousands of years after the civilization perished. But we don't know a lot about this civilization because their script hasn't been deciphered yet!

**291** In 280 B.C., the sculptor Chares of Lindos built a 100 feet high bronze statue of the Sun God Helios. Named the Colossus of Rhodes, it was destroyed in a terrible earthquake in 224 B.C.

**292** Two important things happened in 356 B.C. – to gain immortality, Herostratus burnt the Temple of Artemis, one of the seven wonders of the ancient world. On the same night, Alexander the Great was born!

**293** Who are the boys who were supposedly raised by a she-wolf? Remus and Romulus. It is believed that Romulus later founded the city of Rome.

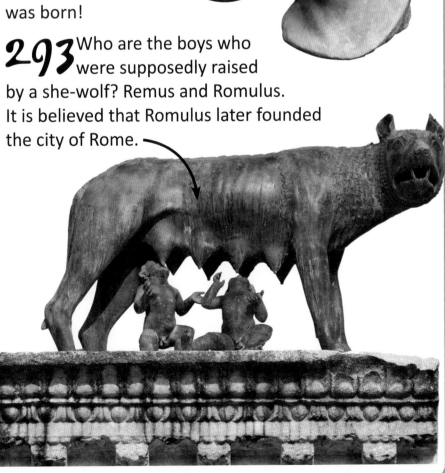

# Medieval World History

**294** Have you heard of Excalibur? Excalibur is the legendary sword that King Arthur pulled from a stone. It is believed that the Excalibur had magical powers which helped King Arthur to defeat his enemies!

**295** Do you know why St Francis of Assisi was canonised in 1628? It was for receiving the stigmata – an unexplained appearance of Christ's wounds on his hands and feet.

**296** Have you heard about the battle of Senlac Hills? You have, but like all of us, you may know it as the Battle of Hastings which was fought between the Norman-French and English armies on 14th October 1066. It should have been called the Battle of Senlac Hills because it was fought there, almost 10 kilometres away from Hastings!

**297** Did you know that the system of a surname was introduced in Britain in 1066? Before that, a person would have just one name and a nickname, so a brown-haired James would be called James Brown, a bald Ted would be called Ted Bald and so on. Gradually, people started retaining the 'nicknames' which eventually became the surname.

**298** Do you know who cleared the path for the Ottoman Empire to rule? It was the Mongols! They invaded Asia Minor in 1243 AD and destroyed the Seljuks.

**299** Viking, in Old Norse, means a pirate raid and that is where the Vikings got their name from. Vikings made their appearance in Europe in the High Middle Ages between AD 700 to 1100. Vikings came from three Scandinavian countries – Denmark, Norway and Sweden.

**300** Heard about the Crusades? The Crusades were a series of religious wars that were fought between the Roman Catholics and the Muslims over a period of 196 years! These were the know as the main Crusades; a number of smaller ones were also fought later.

**301** What is the Silk Road? It is not a road of silk but a trade route developed by Emperor Wudi, that traders used to trade silk from China to the West, and glass, linen and gold from the West to China.

**302** Now a UNESCO World Heritage Site, the Qutub Minar is an object of beauty. Construction started in AD 1192 by Qutubuddin Aibak and completed by Firoz Shah Tughlaq in 1368. The minaret has 379 stairs which takes one to the top floor and gives a complete view of the city of Delhi, India.

# Modern History

**303** There is a surprising event that has occurred only once in modern times. On 29th March 1848, the Niagara Falls stopped flowing for half an hour! Why? Because an ice jam blocked the source of the river.

**305** Just before the start of World War II, the world faced a severe economic depression which was termed the 'Great Depression'. It started in 1929 and lasted until the late 1930's/early 1940's.

**306** The United Nations is probably the most important organisation started in modern times. Founded in 1945, the UN makes decisions about human rights and resolves conflicts. A total of 191 countries are members of the UN.

**307** The famous buccaneer, Captain Blackbeard buried around $1.5 million worth of silver in the mountains outside McKean County. He was to return for the money but the war of 1812 broke out and he could never retrieve it. The silver is still there somewhere!

**304** What is it that you might stumble across in the Bavarian Alps in Austria? A lot of treasure but not ancient treasure! Towards the end of Word War II, the Nazi army buried a large amount of gold, jewels and other priceless objects in the Bavarian Alps so that the Allied Forces would not find them!

**308** Division can be difficult, painful and cause loss of lives, relationships and property. An important event in modern history was the independence of India which resulted in partition and the creation of Pakistan. This division displaced a record 1.24 million people!

PAKISTAN

INDIA

**309** Did you know that the announcement of the end of World War I, was declared on the 11th hour, of the 11th day, of the 11th month, in 1918?

**310** This is a picture of a German Shepherd dog. Do you know the name of the most popular German Shepherd dog? Rin Tin Tin! During the World War I, he was born in a trench in 1918. Rin Tin Tin became a famous dog and starred in more than 40 films.

# Battles and Wars

**311** When invading France during World War I, the Germans did not come from the borders. They took the train to enter the cities instead! The French troops waiting at the border had to be sent back by taxis to counter the attack!

**312** Do you know what were Quaker guns? They were logs made to look like guns or cannons. From a distance, these looked like real guns and made the enemy think that the forces were better equipped than they actually were.

**313** One of the longest and bloodiest battles of all times was the Battle of Stalingrad (World War II). Fought between German and Soviet forces, this battle went on from 19th August 1942 to 2nd February 1943.

**314** You should have heard of the Spanish Armada – the fleet of 130 ships that were sent to attack Britain. Britain not only won the battle, but also put one of the strongest and most powerful navies to shame.

**315** The youngest person to be awarded Britain's highest military honour, the Victoria Cross, was Andrew Fitzgibbon. He was all of 15 when he was awarded the medal for bravery during action at Taku Forts, China, on 21st August, 1860.

**316** What marked the end of Napoleon's Hundred Days after he returned from Elba where he had been exiled? The Battle of Waterloo which was fought between the French under Napoleon's leadership and the allied armies commanded by Gebhard Blucher and the Duke of Wellington.

**317** You may have heard of 'Sherman's Neckties'. What were these? Sherman's neckties were a phenomenon of the American Civil War named after Maj. Gen. William Sherman. The rail tracks were destroyed by heating so they became malleable enough to be twisted around tress – just like a necktie!

**318** After the battle of Hydaspes between Alexander and Porus (Porus lost) in 326 B.C., Porus was captured. When he was brought in front of Alexander, he said something that made Alexander release him. What did he say? Well, when asked how would he want to be treated, Porus answered, 'the way one king would treat another!'

# Myths, Legends & Religions

**319** We all know that the Holy Grail was the cup that Jesus used at the Last Supper. Legend has it that the Holy Grail was taken to England by Joseph of Arimathea but was lost. Since then many people have gone on quests to find it. The legend has featured in many paintings, books and movies.

**320** You may have noticed a feathered serpent in ancient Mayan temples. The feathered serpent is the Mayan God Kukulcán. Some people believe that Kukulcán was later adopted by the Toltecs and Aztecs as Quetzalcoatl.

**321** Thursday is a happy day because it brings us closer to Friday and then the weekend! Do you know where Thursday gets its name from? From Thor – the red-haired and bearded Norse god of war. Thursday from Thor's Day!

**322** The ancient Greeks had three main gods – Zeus, Poseidon and Hades. Zeus ruled the skies, Poseidon ruled the waters and Hades ruled the underworld. They worked with a team of 9 other major gods and goddesses from Mount Olympus, where they lived.

**323** Did you know that Muslims believe that the words of Qur'an, the holy book of the Muslims, are the exact words of Allah as spoken to the messenger Muhammad. It is said that the text hasn't been changed since it first appeared in 632 AD.

**324** Hinduism is the oldest of the world's living religions. Do you know why Ganesha, the Hindu God for prosperity, has an elephant's head? Because his head was cut off in a fight and was replaced by the head of the first creature that was found!

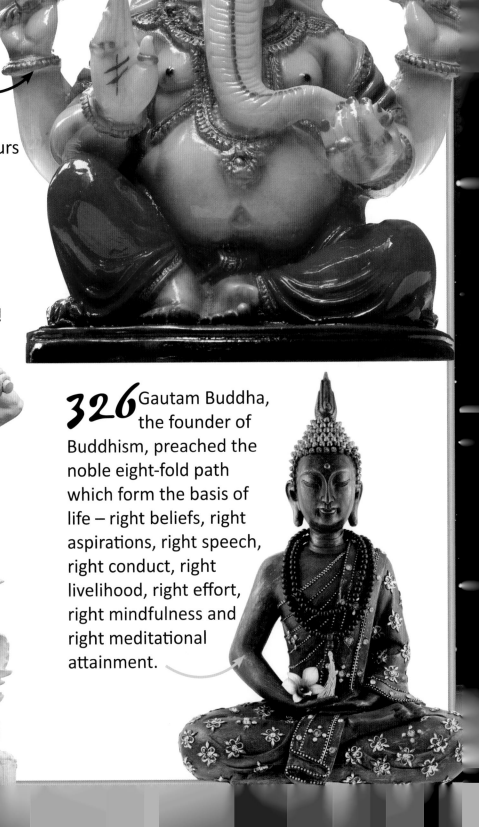

**325** Did you know that Hercules's ten labours were not ten but twelve?! Two of his labours were not considered valid because he took his nephew's help in slaying the Hydra and took a part of land for the task of cleaning the Augean stables!

**326** Gautam Buddha, the founder of Buddhism, preached the noble eight-fold path which form the basis of life – right beliefs, right aspirations, right speech, right conduct, right livelihood, right effort, right mindfulness and right meditational attainment.

# Human Body

**327** Do you know which is the largest organ of the human body? It is the skin and accounts for almost 16 per cent of your body weight!

**328** Talking of body weight, did you know that your skeleton accounts for a fifth of your body weight? So, if your weight is 40 kg, your skeleton weighs 8 kg!

**329** Have you realised the importance of saliva? It helps you to eat your favourite and even the not-so favourite foods! It is estimated that an average person will make 37,800 litres of saliva in their lifetime!

**330** All bones in our body are connected to one another, barring one. The hyoid bone – a U-shaped bone at the base of the tongue – is not connected to any other bone. It gets all the support from the muscles in the neck.

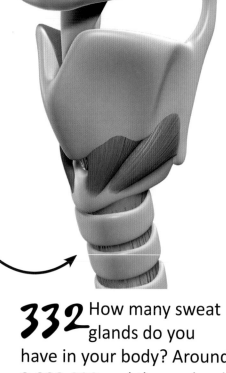

**331** Your eyes provide you with the sense of sight and to keep it working properly, you blink and create tears which clean your eyes and keep them healthy. How many times to do you blink? More than 10,000 times in a day!

**332** How many sweat glands do you have in your body? Around 3,000,000 and these glands excrete around half a litre of water from your body in a day! And in hotter climates, the amount goes up! So, remember to drink a lot of water!

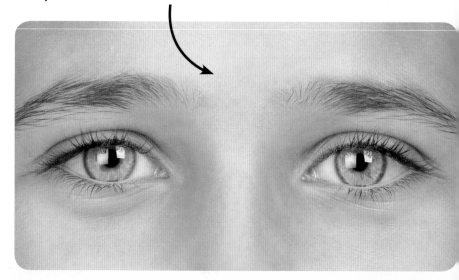

**333** The brain is the most important organ of your body. It controls all your movements and is also the recording system of your body and when you are sleeping, it is busy storing away all the memories you have gained! And did you know that when you are sleeping, it secretes a hormone so that you don't start enacting your dreams!

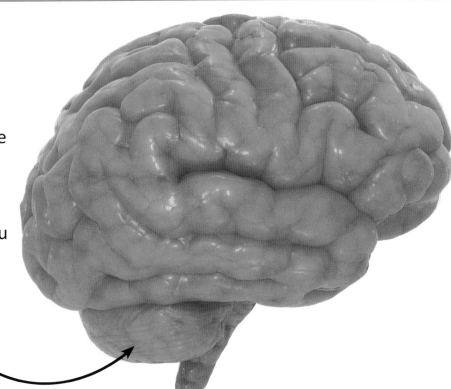

**335** We know that our heart pumps the blood around our body but how many times a day, do you think? In one day, it transports all our blood around the body about a 1000 times!

**334** In 8 hours of sleep, you dream only for about an hour and a half.

# Body Facts and Records

**336** A tummy tuck is not only when you suck in your tummy to hide that little paunch. People tuck their tummies by removing fat surgically. The largest tummy tuck operation performed ever has been on a man in 2010 where a total of 120 kg of fat was removed!

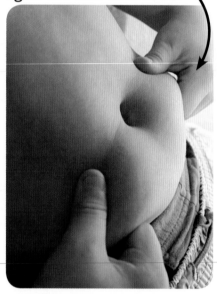

**337** Robert Wadlow had the biggest feet ever! He wore shoes which were a size 37 (US) or 36 (UK)! What size do you wear, 4 or 5? The company that made special shoes for him (which cost $100 in the 1930's) gave them to him for free, and Robert in return did promotional tours for the company.

**338** How long can a tooth be? Well, the average tooth of an average human being would be around 16–18mm, but Loo Hui Jing of Singapore is definitely above average. One of Loo's teeth that was extracted, measured 3.2cm!

**339** Talking of hair, did you know that Sarwan Singh's beard measures 7 feet and 9 inches?! If standing alongside him, his beard would be much taller than him!

**340** Do you think Pinocchio had the longest nose? Think again. Guinness Book of Records has recorded the name of Mehmet Ozyurek to have the longest nose – it is 3.46 inches from bridge to tip!

**341** Stick your tongue out and see how long and wide it is. No matter how wide, it won't be anywhere close to Jay Sloot's tongue that measures 3.1 inches at the widest!

**342** How many times have you been told off for not trimming your nails? Well, not all people get scolded for it. Louise Hollis has the longest toenails in the world. The combined length of all her toenails is 87 inches! And Melvin Boothe is even further ahead of her. He has the longest fingernails in the world which measure 32 feet 3.8 inches!

**343** Did you know that there are some people who suffer from hypertrichosis, commonly known as the werewolf syndrome? People who suffer from this syndrome have hair on all parts of their body except their palms and their feet!

**344** We generally have ten fingers and ten toes with some strange exceptions who have maybe 11 or 12. But there are stranger exceptions. On 19th March 2010, a boy in China was found to have 15 fingers and 16 toes!

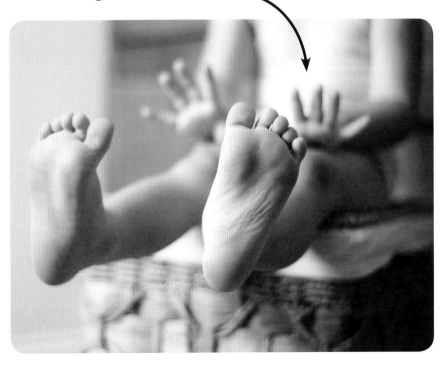

# Extremes!

**345** The tallest hotel in the world is the Rose Rayhaan in Dubai. It measures 333 metres from ground level to the top of its mast. You should find a room for yourself from their 482 rooms spread over 72 floors.

**346** What will you do with these matchsticks? You shouldn't play with them but craftsman Toufic Daher made models. The tallest that he has ever built was a scale replica of the Eiffel Tower. It measured 6 metres and 53 centimetres.

**347** Men with beards is normal, but women with beards is unusual. However, Vivian Elaine Wheeler has a beard which measures 11 inches!

**348** The Danyang-Kunshan Grand Bridge on the Beijing–Shanghai High-Speed Railway is 164 km long. If you were going at a speed of 80 kph, it would take you two hours to cross the bridge. It took 4 years and 10000 people to build.

**349** How much money does your piggy bank hold? Imagine how much money the largest in the world would hold. It is 5.6 m long, 3.96 m tall and has a circumference of 14.6 m! Happy counting!

**350** Did you know that the Grand Mosque in Djenne, Mali, is the largest mud building in the world? Measuring 100 m long and 40 m wide, the mosque was built in 1905!

**351** When did Xie Qiuping last have a haircut? In 1973 when she was all of 13! 39 years later, her hair measures 18 feet and 5.54 inches! Staying away from the hairdresser has been rewarding – there is no other woman in the world with longer hair.

**352** You love sticking stickers? Then you would love to know that the largest sticker measures 63.98 m x 127.26 m (209 ft 10 in x 417 ft 6 in) with a total area of 8,141.84 square metres! If the sticker doesn't boggle your mind, these numbers would!

**353** After 14 years of hard work, on 15th October 2010 the drilling of the longest tunnel in the world was completed - 2000 m beneath the Swiss Alps. When it officially opens in 2016, the 57-km Gotthard Rail Tunnel will take up to 300 trains a day!

# Extreme Price - Most Expensive

**354** A wedding gown worth $12 million adorned with 150 carats' worth of diamonds was created for a show in 2006 by Martin Katz Jewellers and Renee Strauss.

**356** If a watch has 66.16 carats of diamonds – 288 trapeze-cut diamonds, 16 centre-stones and 1,897 brilliant-cut diamonds – how much do you think it would cost? $1,130,620! Super Ice Cube by Chopard is the most expensive watch.

**355** Ignore the wedding dress and read this – the most expensive wedding to-date is that of Vanisha Mittal, daughter of billionaire Lakshmi Mittal, to Amit Bhatia. A wedding that cost $55 million and was held at the Palace of Versailles doesn't need any more, does it?

**357** How much would you pay for a haircut? Does a few pounds or dollars sound reasonable? An Italian customer paid Stuart Philips £8,000 ($16,420) for a haircut on 29th October 2007.

90

**358** Look before you spray that perfume because it might cost a fortune! Like the limited edition of the Clive Christian No. 1 Collection which costs $205,000 for a mere 500ml!

**359** How much would a pair of jeans cost? The pair called Swarovski Crystal Jeans made by Escada cost only $10,000! Studded with Swarovski crystals, this is the most expensive jeans available commercially.

**360** How much is this 'regular' Tibetan mastiff worth? An 11 month old red Tibetan mastiff was sold for 10 million Chinese yuan ($1,513,417) in March 2011. Who says a dog's life is cheap!

**361** Gordon Ramsey's Maze restaurant in the UK serves the most expensive pizza in the world at £100 each! What 'special' topping does it have? Well along with the regular stuff, it is garnished with fresh shavings of a rare Italian white truffle, which itself costs £1,400 per kilogram!

# Extreme Food

**362** If you are going to the Serendipity 3 restaurant in New York and planning to order a dessert, think before you order their 'Frrrozen Haute Chocolate ice cream sundae' because you will need to pay a whopping $25,000 for it!

**363** Do you like chocolates? Then you will like Amedei Porcelana, world's most expensive chocolate. But you might not like the price – $90 for 450 grams!

**364** Did you know that Nick Moraitis of Australia paid $35000 (Australian dollars) for a box of cherries on 24 October 2007? So much for your 5-a-day!

**365** The people at Lawson Inc., Japan, love pasta as much as anyone. In 2010 they managed to make a pasta strand that measured 3,776 metres! If this is not love, then what is?

**366** The world's most expensive food is 'Almas', from the Iranian Beluga fish. Just a kilogram of it is sold for £20,000. You could buy a car for that amount!

**367** We love the Lebanese dish, hummus, but how much of it can you eat in one go? No matter how much you like it, you can't polish the largest serving of hummus off – as it weighs 23,130 kilograms!

**368** Baskin Robbins is sure in demand if Mitch Cohen (of Baskin-Robbins New York) can scoop 19 ice cream cones in a minute! That's a world record!

**369** Salad is healthy, when eaten in the right quantity. But the largest salad ever weighed 13,417 kg when it was made in Greece on 19th June 2010. Healthy, I am not sure, but a world record holder it definitely is.

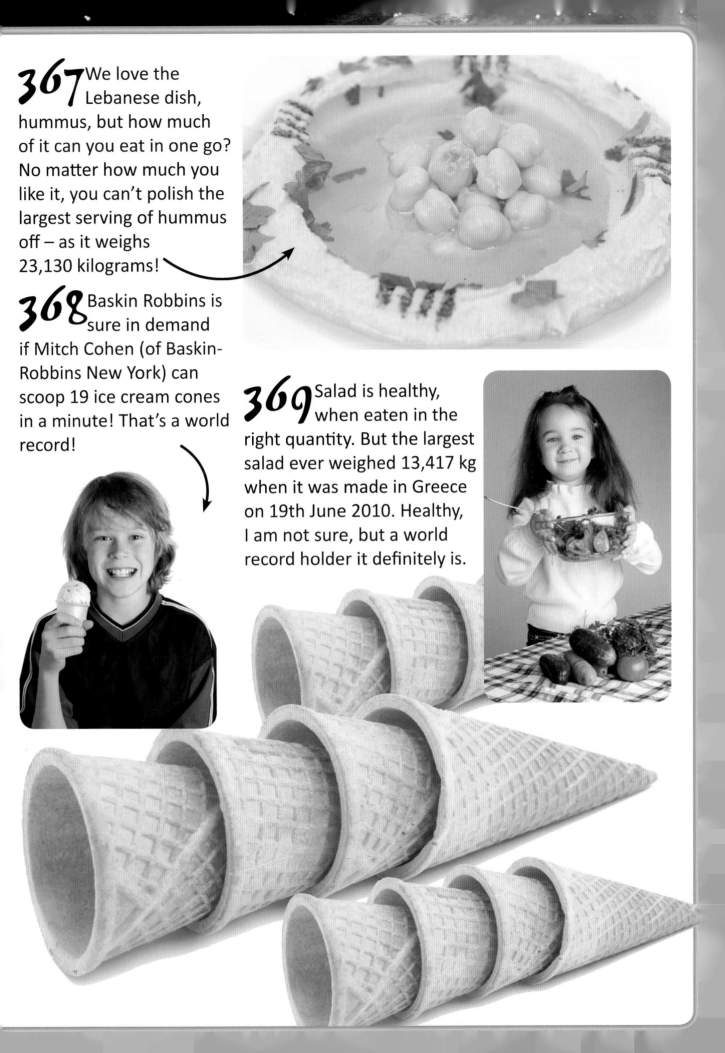

# Extreme People!

**370** We live in a world of extremes and this one is about extreme weight. The heaviest man ever was Jon Brower Minnoch, who weighed – not 200, not 300 – but 635 kilograms! Minnoch died in 1983 of congestive heart failure.

**371** And when it comes to making records, women do not fall 'short'. The shortest mobile living woman is Jyoti Amge of Nagpur, India. Jyoti is so small at 62.8cm that she is less that the height of an umbrella.

**372** Women live longer than men! How do we know that? Records show that on 20th February 2010, 76 people were authenticated to be over the age of 110 and only 3 of the 76 were men!

**373** Women are generally very particular about their curves but not all. Rosalie Bradford (1943–2006) was one of those who didn't care much about 'weighty' issues. At 544 kilograms, she couldn't be curvier.

**374** The oldest living man award goes to Jiroemon Kimura of Japan. Born on 19th April 1897, Kimura celebrated his 114th birthday in 2011.

**375** Shigetsugu Anan (83 years 11 days) and his wife Miyoko Anan (78 years 71 days) are the oldest couple to run a marathon on 13 January 2008 in Japan!

**376** Together the longest! Herbert Fisher (USA, b. 10 June 1905) and Zelmyra Fisher (USA, b. 10 December 1907) were married on May 13, 1924 and have been married now for more than 87 years!

**377** The shortest living mobile man is Junrey Balawing of the Philippines who measures just 2.35 inches under 2 feet! But Balawing is less than an inch taller than Gul Mohammad (1957-1997) of India, who at 22.5 inches, is the shortest man ever.

# Dinosaurs and Other Extinct Animals

**378** The largest prehistoric mammal was indricotherium – a long-necked, hornless rhinocerotid. It was 37 feet long and measured 17 feet 9 inches high to the shoulder hump.

**379** How long can a tusk be? A mastodon tusk measuring 16 feet 6 inches was excavated in 2007 in Greece. That's quite a length.

**380** You must be wondering how the word 'dinosaur' made an appearance. As these animals looked like 'terrible lizards', Richard Owen suggested the name 'dinosauria' in July 1841 and the name has stuck ever since.

**381** The dodo never learnt to fly because it never needed to run away from any predators until it met man. And that led to its extinction as it couldn't easily escape human hunters. The last if them was seen around 1681.

**382** The sabre-toothed tiger wasn't really a tiger. It belonged to a genus of a prehistoric cat called the Smilodon. The Smilodon were distant relatives of tigers, lions and cheetahs.

**383** The woolly mammoth was a close relative of the elephant and became extinct as 'recently' as 4,000 years ago. Some of their remains have been found 'almost intact' in Siberia's permafrost. These animals were hunted to extinction by early humans!

**384** Though none of us has ever seen a dinosaur, it is undeniable that it is the most famous animal of all times. The dinosaurs appeared 230 million years ago and disappeared around 65 million years ago. The first dinosaurs to be described were the Megalosaurus and Iguanodon. This was even before the word 'dinosaur' was used.

**385** Do you know which creature is called a living fossil? The coelacanth. These fish lived at the same time as dinosaurs and scientists believed that they had become extinct too but were rediscovered on 22nd December 1938.

**386** Our penguins are not 'original penguins' because that name was originally given to the great auks that became extinct in the mid-19th century. They were killed for food, bait, feathers, and fat.

# Fossils

**387** Do you know the name of the first aquatic reptile that existed? It's the Mesosaurus which lived between 320–280 million years ago! And how do we know this? Through fossil, records!

**389** One of the oldest and most important fossil bed formations in the world is the Burgess Shale formation in Canada. It was formed about 530 million years ago during the Cambrian period.

**391** Not only animal bones were preserved in fossilized form, but even plants were! How else would we know that a plant called 'cooksonia', the earliest vascular land plant, existed some 425 million years ago!

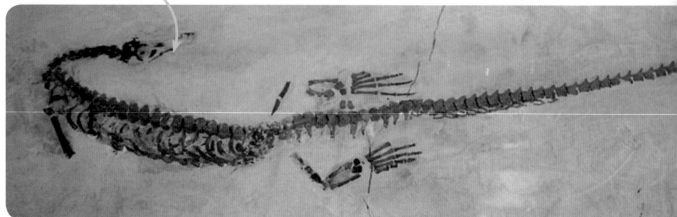

**388** Pterosaurs were the largest flying prehistoric creatures. The study of pterosaur fossil shows that the wings of Quetzalcoatlus, the biggest pterosaur, measured 10.96 metres from one tip to the other!

**390** Did you know that the size of all the prehistoric animals are generally estimated by the size of legs and others bones that are preserved in fossilized form? The largest known complete skeleton fossil found so far is that of a Brachiosaurus dinosaur. If you are in Berlin, Germany, you can have a look at the skeleton in the Humboldt Museum.

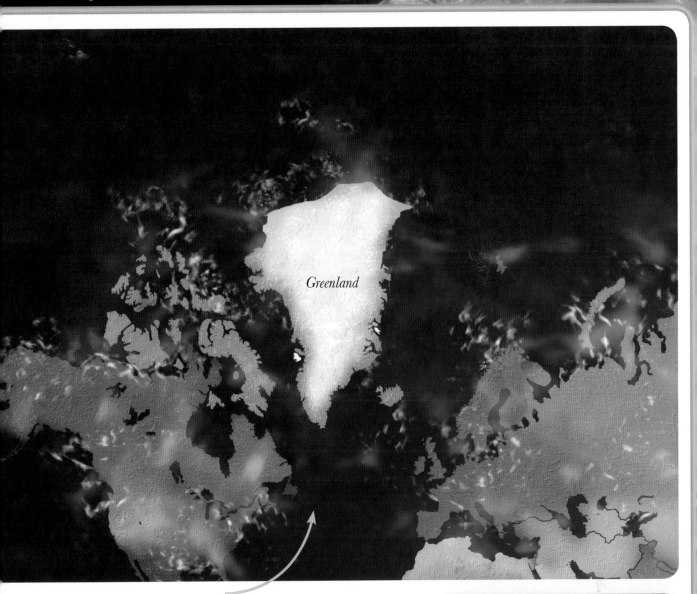

*Greenland*

**392** Do you know what the earliest fossil records tell us? They show that microscopic life forms existed as long ago as 3,700 to 3,800 million years. This evidence was found in Isua greenstone in Greenland.

**393** Now that we are talking about fossils, you should know that the people who study and tell us about these fossils are called palaeontologists.

**394** Have you been into space? No? Dinosaurs have! In 1985, astronaut Loren Acton took some fragments of bones and eggshell of Maiasaura peeblesorum into space. Years later in 1998, astronaut Bonnie Dunbar took the skull of the Coelophysis into space for scientific research!

# Mammals

**395** We know that elephants are heavy, very heavy, and because of all that weight, they can't jump! A baby elephant can drink 80 litres of milk in a day, imagine how much would an adult eat!

**397** We all know that mammals give birth to live young and other animals types lay eggs. But there are a few mammals that lay eggs! They are called monotremes. The duck-billed platypus and echidna are two examples.

**399** Did you know that the koala bear has fingerprints like us? So do gorillas but surprisingly not chimpanzees! It is difficult to explain why some do and others don't!

**396** Lions live in groups called prides. And the dominant male lion is the head of the group – the task of providing for food falls to the female lions, but the male usually gets to eat first!

**398** Did you know that the ivory tusk of the male narwhal grows to a length of approximately 2 metres? But that's normal. The bigger ones can go up to 3 metres and weigh around 10 kg!

**400** Man is the cleverest mammal. We all know that, but who comes next? The chimpanzee! The chimp is followed by the gorilla, orang-utan, baboon, gibbon and monkey!

**401** Do you know the name of the largest nocturnal primate? It is strangely called Aye Aye. And how large is it? The body length is 40 cm and the tail is longer by 10.5 cm! Aye aye!

**402** We know that the cheetah can run at a speeds up to 100 kph and that is the fastest land animal but did you know that it only has the record of the fastest land mammal over a short distance. The fastest land animal over long distance is the pronghorn!

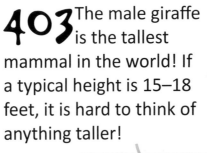

**403** The male giraffe is the tallest mammal in the world! If a typical height is 15–18 feet, it is hard to think of anything taller!

# Birds

**404** You may not have seen parakeets eating chillies, but they can without any trouble at all! That is because birds are not sensitive to capsaicin, the hot stuff in chillies. We are, aren't we!

**405** The Arctic tern is a migratory bird. But what distance do you think it migrates every year, 1000 kilometres or 2000 kilometres? No, it migrates all the way from the Arctic to the Antarctic and back – a total distance of 71000 kilometres!

**406** We may know that the ostrich is a bird that can't fly and we also know that it lays very big eggs. But how big? Around 2.35 kg! This is as heavy as a human baby!

**407** Did you know that some birds, such as flamingos, have strainers built in to their beaks? This means they have the ability to filter their food – they eat what they need and leave out what they don't need.

**408** The bat is a strange creature that flies but it is not a bird! It is a mammal. It loves to hand upside down on cave walls during the day and hunt for food at night. That makes the bat a nocturnal, flying mammal.

**409** Do you know what is special about the common poorwill? No, not that it has a strange name! It is the only bird that hibernates to escape extreme cold temperatures!

**410** Do you know that in 1973, a bird was recorded flying at 11,273 metres above sea level? That was 2,425 metres above Mount Everest! And the bird was Ruppell's griffon vulture. It goes without saying that it is the highest flying bird.

**411** The cuckoo is a strange bird. It lays its eggs in the nest of other birds, such as the crow, and the crow raises it as its own! This is called brood-parasitism. Think of it as passing off responsibility!

**412** Frigatebirds are amazing creatures! They can't walk or swim but when it comes to flying, they can fly endlessly for weeks at a time! The most interesting feature is displayed by the male of the species during the mating season. To attract females, they display a red gular sac (like a red balloon) that connects the neck to the beak!

# Reptiles

**413** Tuataras are similar to lizards, but they are not the same. They are the only surviving members of a group of reptiles called 'sphenodontids' which thrived at the time of the dinosaurs!

**415** Did you know that not all reptiles live on land? The marine iguana and also many sea snakes, live in water.

**414** Did you know that the blood-squirting toad is not a toad but a lizard? Yes, it is actually a short-horned lizard. When threatened by an enemy, it squirts blood from its eyes! Some defence mechanism!

**416** We have always thought of crocodiles, caimans, gharials and alligators as big creatures, but not all of them are huge. The dwarf caiman is actually small, and males do not go beyond 1.5 m and the female barely gets to 1.2 m, fully grown.

**417** Do you know one very special thing about chameleons – they can stretch their tongue three times the length of their body to catch food!

**418** Losers can be winners too. If you don't believe it, just look at the turtles. They are slow and heavy on land but in water, they are fast and streamlined. The Pacific leatherback turtle can swim at a speed of 35 kph making it one of the fastest animals in the sea!

**419** What is the largest lizard? It is the Komodo Dragon. Imagine a lizard that weighs up to 70kg! Also it was discovered only in 2009 at Melbourne University, Australia, that it is venomous too!

**421** Snakes are venomous creatures and we are all scared of them, lest they bite us and we die, right? But studies show that in the US, four times more people die of wasp and bee stings than snake bites!

**420** Regarding snakes, the longest venomous snake is the king cobra, which is found in southeast Asia and India. One bite is enough to bring down a large elephant! It can grow to between 12–15 feet long.

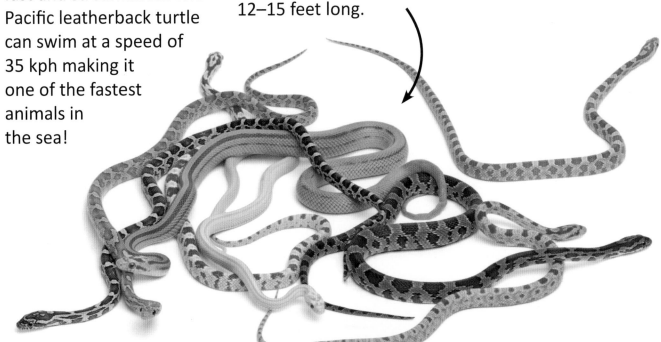

# Amphibians

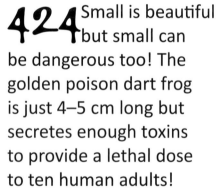

**421** How interesting would it be to be able to live on land as well as in water? Amphibians can, and the largest is the Chinese giant salamander. One specimen collected was as long as 5 feet 11 inches and weighed almost 65 kg!

**422** You may be able to guess why 'glass frogs' are so named – because their abdominal skin is partially transparent. If you see them from beneath, you can see their heart, liver and stomach!

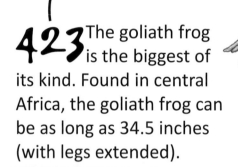

**423** The goliath frog is the biggest of its kind. Found in central Africa, the goliath frog can be as long as 34.5 inches (with legs extended).

**424** Small is beautiful but small can be dangerous too! The golden poison dart frog is just 4–5 cm long but secretes enough toxins to provide a lethal dose to ten human adults!

**425** Amphibians are divided into three groups – toads and frogs, newts, and finally salamanders and caecilians. Caecilians are limbless creatures that resemble earthworms. Their most amazing physical feature is their eyes which are hidden beneath a layer of skin.

**426** Do you know what is so special about the yellow-spotted bell frog? For many years it was considered extinct, but fortunately in 2010 a thriving colony was found in Australia!

**427** Did you know that the North American Wood Frog 'freezes' to stay alive?! To survive the cold winters, this frog surrounds its organs with freezing water. It stays that way until the weather changes and then 'thaws' out and springs back to life!

**428** You can't hear the concave-eared torrent frog croak! Why? Because it croaks at so high a pitch that it is beyond the range of human hearing. We can hear up to 20 kHz whereas this frog emits a croak at 128 kHz.

**429** Frogs have body odour and some just pretend to have it! The 'smelliest' of them is the Venezuela skunk frog. To warn off predators, it releases a chemical which is similar to the smell produced by a skunk!

# Sea Creatures

**430** Did you know that a black marlin fish can lay as many as 226 million eggs at a time!

**431** What is so special about the Barramundi fish? It is sequentially hermaphroditic – it is born a male and after one spawning season, it turns into a female. However, not all males will turn into females.

**432** Why are dumbo octopuses so called? Not because they are stupid, but because their ears resemble those of Walt Disney's flying elephant Dumbo! What a name!

**434** Why is it that you keep feeding your lovely goldfish and it keeps eating without stopping? That's so because goldfish have a memory span of 3 to 5 seconds and they forget they have eaten as soon as they eat!

**433** Piranhas are dangerous creatures! They are ferocious fish that live in rivers in parts of South America. They hunt in groups and attack anything they can – even humans who come close! Within minutes, piranhas strip their prey to the bone with their sharp teeth.

**435** The biggest sea creature is the whale and the biggest of the whales is the blue whale. But it is not a fish, it is a mammal that lives in water. On average, a blue whale weighs as much as 25 elephants put together, which would be close to 170, 000 kilograms!

**436** An elephant takes 22 months to deliver a child but that's not the longest pregnancy of all creatures. The longest is that of the common frilled shark – she stays pregnant for 3.5 years!

**437** You may have seen many deep-sea divers in films, but have you ever seen a 'natural' deep-sea diver? Leatherback turtles dive to great depths. In 1987, one of them was recorded diving to a depth of 1200 metres!

**438** A stonefish is so called because they lie on the seabed and resemble stones. But they are not as harmless as a stone and if an unsuspecting swimmer steps on them, they receive a painful sting from their spines. These stings can be fatal!

# Insects and Arachnids

**439** Did you know that male mosquitoes don't bite? They don't need blood as they survive on water and plant juice. Those bites on your body are all due to female mosquitoes who have found a blood donor in you!

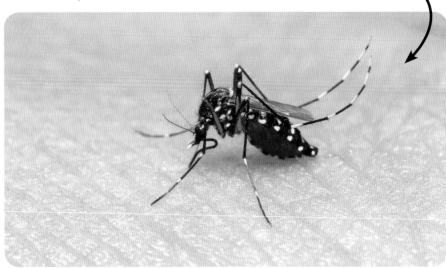

**440** You should already know that honeybees make food not only for themselves but also for us! They feed their young with honey and whatever remains, we harvest! And not just honey, we also use beeswax for making candles and polish.

**441** How big can a butterfly's wingspan be? Well, the wings of the Queen Alexandria's Birdwing butterfly of Papua New Guinea measures 28 centimetres across! That's quite some size!

**442** The largest bees are Wallace's giant bees. They can be as big as 4 centimetres. First found in 1858 in Indonesia, these bees were thought to be extinct for many years till they were rediscovered in 1981.

**443** We all hate houseflies, don't we? And we think they seem to live forever as they are always in the house, but in reality they live short lives. A male housefly lives for 17 days and a female for 29 days!

**444** Have you heard of the bombardier beetle? The bombardier beetle has an amazing defence mechanism! When threatened by an enemy, the beetle swings its tail and 'bombards' the enemy with a noxious fluid! The liquid is also very hot, as well as corrosive!

**445** I'm sure you didn't think that only humans are noisy, because insects are noisy too! The noisiest being colonies of hundreds of male cicadas that make loud noises to attract females. They can get as loud as the noise from heavy traffic!

**447** We all know that locusts fly around in swarms and that the swarms are huge - but how huge? Estimates say that one swarm of locusts usually contains up to 50 billion insects. In fact, one such swarm seen in 1889 is estimated to have had 250 billion locusts and to have weighed half a million tonnes!

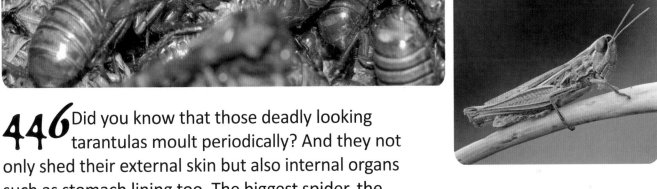

**446** Did you know that those deadly looking tarantulas moult periodically? And they not only shed their external skin but also internal organs such as stomach lining too. The biggest spider, the goliath birdeater, is also a tarantula!

# Endangered Animals

**448** Have you ever seen a tarsier? Doesn't it look cute with such large eyes and a cuddly body? But what is interesting about this primate is the fact that it spends almost all its life attached to a tree trunk – even whilst sleeping and giving birth.

**450** Did you know that the double-humped Bactrian camel can drink up to 135 litres of water in only 13 minutes?! However the humps are actually fat stores!

**451** Did you know that a giant panda is not born big? In fact it is born far too small to be called giant. A newborn panda is barely the size of a slab of butter – almost 1/900th of its mother's size!

**449** Did you know that Royal Bengal Tigers make up about half of all wild tigers? These huge creatures can eat up to 27 kilograms of food at a time and if you look closely you will notice that no two have the same stripes.

**455** Giant otters have been known to feed on fish, small snakes and crustacean - this is common knowledge. But did you know that giant otters have been seen feeding on small caimans!

**456** The Asiatic cheetah is extinct in India and only a few of them can be spotted in Central Iran. There was a time when thousands could be seen between the Arabian Sea and India. In fact, the name 'cheetah' is derived from the Sanskrit word 'chitraka' meaning 'the spotted one'.

**452** You may not know that the ghariyal's scientific name is Gavialis gangeticus. But this name is also based upon a misspelling of the Hindi word 'ghariyal' (which is what it is actually called in India)! If the scientists had gotten the name right, then it would probably have been known as Ghariyalis gangeticus!

**453** Time for some mathematics again – how many krill does a blue whale eat in a day if one krill weighs 1-2 grams and a blue whale eats anywhere between eight to ten tons of krill! Millions!

**454** Do you know when the Tasmanian devil yawns? Not when it is sleepy, but when it is confronted by an enemy – it yawns to show its teeth rather than that it is not bothered by the threat!

# Pets and Cattle!

**457** Pets too, can be record breakers. For example, Puggy is a nine-year-old Pekingese dog whose tongue measures a record 4.5 inches! He would be great at licking his bowl clean!

**458** A dog's life can be nice. It is at 'Barkingham Palace' the most expensive kennels in the world. Each kennel has a plasma television, retina-controlled dog flap and everything else that a dog could wish for!

**459** When it comes to breaking records, cats don't let dogs have all the fun. Cream Puff, a female cat, was born on 3rd August 1967 and lived till 6th August 2005 – 38 years and 3 days!

**460** Talking about cats, the tallest domestic cat is a Savannah cross. Named Scarlet's Magic, this cat measured 16.48 inches in 2009. She may even have grown more since then!

the longest rabbit in the world at an amazing 4 feet 3 inches long! I wonder how high he can jump?

**461** Now it's time for some rabbit news. Flemish giant rabbits are big. But Darius beats all his brothers and sisters. He is

**462** Now here is some information about goldfish – the oldest goldfish ever was Tish who lived for more than 43 years! The owner had 'won' the goldfish in a fairground stall in 1956 and the fish stayed with the owner's family until it finally died in 1999.

**463** If you love horse riding, you still may not want to ride Big Jake. Not for any other reason than for his sheer size, and at 82.5 inches (without shoes, that is!) Big Jake is a walking 'mountain'.

**464** This one is for all animal lovers – Laucidio Coelho owned a farm in Mato Grosso, Brazil, that spread over an area of 8,700 square kilometres. At the time of Coelho's death in 1975, the farm supported a record 250,000 cattle!

# World Languages

**465** Do you know which is the most commonly spoken language? Do you think its English? No, it is not. The most common language is actually Chinese spoken by 1.1 billion people worldwide!

**468** And when it comes to different alphabets, the one with the maximum of letters is Khmer (Cambodian). It has 74 letters!

**466** Which language is spoken in the most number of countries? What you had probably guessed for the previous question is the right answer this time – English! English is spoken in at least 57 countries followed by French in 33!

**467** The Chinese do not have an alphabet but use a system of symbols to write? How many symbols do they have? Well, some large dictionaries have up to 50,000 characters but in order to read a newspaper, you would need to know at least 2000-3000 characters! That's a lot more than our 26!

**469** How many words per minute can you read? 70 or 80? A skilled Braille reader (Braille is a system of raised dots that allow the blind to read) can read up to 150 words in a minute!

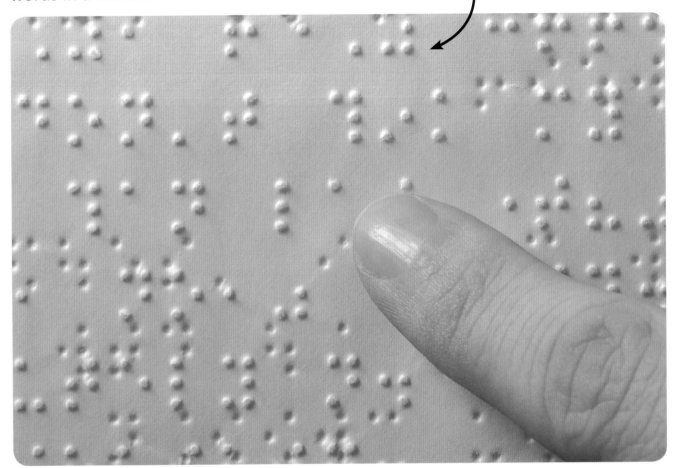

**470** Which is the oldest surviving European alphabet? It is the Greek alphabet. Did you know that initially Greek was written from right to left but around 500 B.C., it was changed and is now left to right.

Α Β Γ Δ Ε Ζ Η Θ
Ι Κ Λ Μ Ν Ξ Ο Π
Ρ Σ Τ Υ Φ Χ Ψ Ω

α β γ δ ε ζ η θ
ι κ λ μ ν ξ ο π ρ
ς σ τ υ φ χ ψ ω

**471** What is the phonetic alphabet? Also known as the NATO phonetic alphabet (it was designed by NATO), it is the most widely used spelling alphabet where words are assigned to each letter so that radio messages can be clearly pronounced and received.

# Plants

**472** Ricin is deadlier than a snake's venom and even a small dosage can kill a person. You must be wondering where is it found. It is extracted from the seeds of the castor oil plant!

**473** Do you know why the Scarlet Pimpernel flower is called the poor man's weatherglass? Because it can forecast the weather! If it is about to rain, the flower will close up and if it is going to be sunny, it will stay open.

**474** Did you know that the General Sherman giant sequoia in Sequoia National Park, California is the world's largest living thing? It is 83.8 metres tall and contains more than enough wood to make shelves for over a million books!

**475** How tall is the tallest tree? Three times the size of the Statue of Liberty! The tallest tree currently growing is Hyperion, which is 115.54 metres tall. It was discovered on 25th August 2006 in the Redwood National Park, California, USA.

**476** Can a tree be a national monument? Well, this one is. A cypress tree known as Sarv-e-Abarkooh in Abarkooh, Iran is estimated to be more than 4,000 years old. No wonder it is a national monument.

**477** Why is the Rafflesia flower called the corpse flower? Because when it blooms, it releases a foul smell which is similar to that of rotting flesh. But, it shares the 'corpse' nickname with the Titan Arum, which is the smelliest flower of the world. And Rafflesia is the largest.

**478** Carnivorous plants trap their prey in very fast movements, so fast that before you know, the prey is gone! Of all the carnivorous plants, the fastest is the Venus Flytrap that traps its prey in one-tenth of a second.

**479** Cigarette smoking is hazardous to health and one should never smoke. Cigarettes contain nicotine, which is a drug found in the tobacco plant. It is actually toxic and 50 milligrams can kill an adult person.

# Sports

**480** The oldest continuous sporting event is Doggett's Coat and Badge Race. This rowing contest has been held on the River Thames since 1715. It is interesting to know that the Newmarket Town Plate horse race is older (it was first held in 1665) but it was discontinued for a while.

**481** Do you love watching TV? What show do you like? Records show that many people love FIFA because the 2006 FIFA World Cup held in Germany between 9th June and 9th July 2006 was the most watched live sporting event on television. FIFA claims that the tournament was seen by 30 billion viewers over that period!

**482** It is believed that athletics is the oldest amongst all the sports. It is difficult to tell the exact date but it is estimated that it goes back to at least 3800 B.C. Well, it is not old but ancient.

**483** Time for some strange sporting events – a world championship in mobile phone throwing! Yes, that's right. It has been held in Finland ever since 2000. The current world record was set in 2002. What's the record? The winner threw his phone a record 66.72 metres!

**484** Many people run in a marathon, but the maximum that have run a marathon to-date is a record 38,706! These people all ran the Boston Marathon centenary race in 1996.

**485** What do you think is the origin of basketball? Well, the inspiration could be the Aztec game 'ollamalitzli' and some other ball and hoop games that South American people played hundreds of years ago! Though the current version was invented in 1891 by Dr James A Naismith.

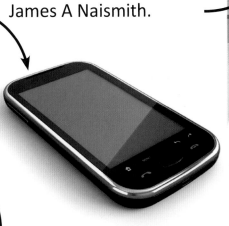

# Sports Records!

**486** Did you know that Muttiah Muralitharan has taken the most number of wickets in his playing career. Overall, 1315 wickets in 17 years. The records of most wickets taken in a Test career (792 wickets) and most wickets taken in ODIs (512 wickets) belong to Muralitharan.

**487** Now to motor-racing. Michael Schumacher has won the most number of Formula One Grand Prix races. But how many exactly? 91 in fourteen years between 1992 and 2006.

**488** We love pool, don't we? And many youngsters around the world play it. The youngest to win the World Championship is Chian-ching Wu of Taiwan. When he won the title on 10th June 2005, he was all of 16 years and 121 days old!

**489** What is the most number of times that the same person has won the tennis Grand Slam singles title? Well, a record 16, by none other than Roger Federer.

**491** Here is an award for bad behaviour on the field – the most number of yellow cards received by a player in the English Premier league is 93! And that's a record you should not try to beat!

**492** Do you know that darts also has a Grand Prix title? And the individual dart player who has won the most number of Grand Prix titles is Phil Taylor of UK. Between 1998 and 2009, he won the title a record nine times.

# Miscellaneous

**493** Have you noticed any statues of men on horses? Did you know that if the horse's front legs are in the air, the person died in battle. If only one leg is in the air, the person died due to wounds received in battle. And if all four are on the ground, the person died of natural causes.

**494** Where do we get the expression 'mind your P's and Q's' from? In English pubs, alcohol was ordered in pints and quarts. And when drunk, customers became unruly, and the bartender would yell at them saying, 'mind your pints and quarts!' Pints and Quarts – P's and Q's!

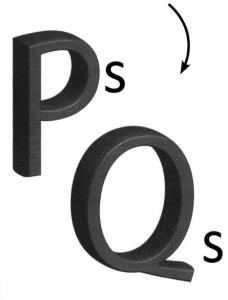

**495** Talking about expressions, where does the expression 'raining cats and dogs' come from? Back in old days, houses in England had thatched roofs with no wood underneath. Since that was a place an animal could stay warm, all the pets of the house would go up there to rest.. When it rained, the roof got slippery and the pets – generally cats and dogs – slipped from the roof!

**499** Extending the arm uses four muscles and smiling takes two, but frowning uses 42 muscles! So, the next time someone irritates you, you know what to do, don't you?

**496** Do you know that each king in a pack of cards represents a great king in history? Spades – King David; Hearts – Charlemagne; Clubs – Alexander, The Great; Diamonds – Julius

Caesar.

**497** Did you know that archaeologists found a golden razor in Tutankhamen's tomb? Even after almost 3000 years, the razor was still sharp enough to use!

**498** Every time you buy something, the person at the counter scans a barcode and all

the information about the product appears on the till. Do you know which was the first product the barcode appeared on? Wrigley's chewing gum!

**499** Well, you know that the Earth is divided into longitudes and latitudes. So, if you wanted to start from zero and stood at 0° longitude and 0° latitude, where would you be? Somewhere in the Atlantic Ocean!

**500** Did you know that the numbers 111, 222, 333, 444, 555, 666, 777, 888, 999 are all multiples of 37?

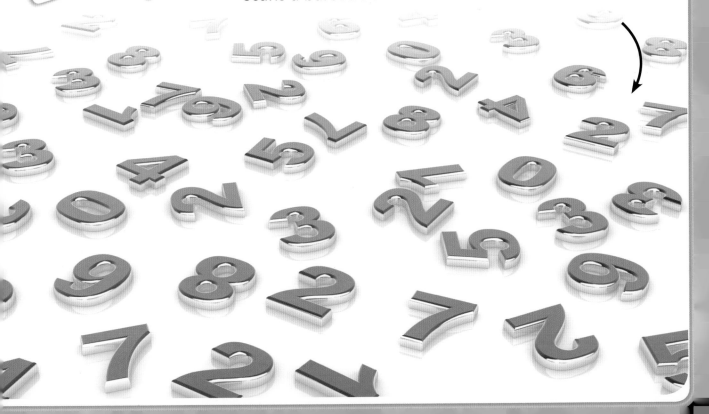